HOW TO WRITE COMPLAINT LETTERS THAT WORK

A Consumer's Guide to Resolving Conflicts & Getting Results

How to Write Complaint Letters That Work

©1994 Park Avenue Publications

An Imprint of JIST Works, Inc.
720 North Park Avenue
Indianapolis, IN 46202-3431
Phone 317-264-3720 • Fax 317-264-3709

Library of Congress Cataloging-in-Publication Data

Westheimer, Patricia H.
  How to write complaint letters that work! : a guide to one of the best methods of resolving conflicts & getting results / Patricia H. Westheimer & Jim Mastro.

    p. cm.
    ISBN 1-57112-063-7 : $12.95
1. Consumer complaints.   2. Complaint letters.   I. Mastro, Jim.
II. Title.   III. Title: Complaint letters that work.
HF5414.5.W47   1994
381.3'3—dc20   94-13780
                                                                CIP

99 98 97 96 95 94   1 2 3 4 5 6 7 8 9

Cover Design: Robert Steven Pawlak

This publication is designed to provide accurate and authoritative information in regard to the subject matter covered. It is sold with the understanding that the publisher is not engaged in rendering legal, accounting or other professional service. If legal advice or other expert assistance is required, the services of a competent professional person should be sought. From a declaration of principles jointly adopted by a committee of the American Bar Association and a committee of publishers.

ISBN 1-57112-063-7

CONTENTS

3

4

5

6

7

8

9

10

PREFACE

The enthusiasm that greeted our call for complaint letters was overwhelming. We collected dozens of actual letters and used as many as possible. Most of the letters reproduced in this book are authentic, each one telling its writer's unique story. However, in order to protect the privacy of both author and recipient, all names, dates, and addresses have been changed. Any resemblance to an actual person, place, or time is purely coincidental.

We welcome this opportunity to thank the following people: Amy Davis, our gracious, helpful, and professional editor; Allen Yarowsky for his friendship, support, and invaluable critical comments; Julius Westheimer for more than can be briefly stated; and good friend Sara Baldwin.

We also wish to thank Lisa Gaudet for her support, encouragement, and understanding, and Steve Kottmeier for his understanding and crucial technical support.

Finally, we wish to thank all those who graciously volunteered the use of their creative complaint letters. In particular, we thank Joan Salb for her letters and professional help, and Don Nagle for his letters, sage advice, and interesting stories.

INTRODUCTION

You've just purchased a new telephone answering machine on sale. You set it up according to the instructions, but you discover that it's defective—it refuses to answer the phone. So you put it back in its box and take it back to the store for a replacement, only to be told that there are no refunds or exchanges for sale items.

You explain, as patiently as possible, the nature of the problem and the fact that you paid good money for a piece of faulty merchandise. The salesperson won't budge, nor will the store manager when you finally get him out of his office. Vowing never to shop at that store again, you storm out, return home, and toss the worthless machine in the garbage, kissing your hard-earned money good-bye. For the next week you complain about shoddy merchandise and the lack of customer service these days. Finally, you reluctantly accept the fact that the system has ripped you off again. Right?

Wrong!

Too many people are willing to accept poor service, defective merchandise, and outright thievery by retail outlets, service organizations, professionals, and landlords. How many times have you been mistreated or overcharged? How many times, as in the example above, have you tried to return defective merchandise only to have salespeople tell you there is nothing they can do? "It's company policy," they say.

Too many people seem willing to accept the maxim "Let the buyer beware!"

The authors of this book *do not* accept that premise. The fact is, retail stores and service organizations—any company or individual that takes money for products or services—cannot survive with a dissatisfied clientele. To paraphrase Peter Finch in the movie *Network:* You don't have to take it anymore! You *can* do something about poor service, rude workers, and inferior merchandise.

Writing and sending a well-crafted complaint letter is the first step. You'll be venting your anger and frustration in a positive and constructive way—and taking a big step toward asserting your rights as a consumer. Chances are your grievances will be addressed to your satisfaction: you'll obtain your refund, replacement, or even greater compensation for your inconvenience or loss.

You, as consumer, have a great deal more power than you might think. The trick is to exercise that power wisely and effectively. With a few well-chosen words in a carefully designed letter addressed to the right person, you can correct almost any wrong, inconvenience, or loss of money or time due to poor service or faulty merchandise.

And this book tells you how—how to make yourself heard in a way that gets results. Through simple, easy-to-understand steps you'll learn how to write effective letters and send them to the person who can do the most to solve your problem.

The days of "Sorry, your warranty is up" or "No refunds" are over!

Why Complain? The Logic Behind the Squeaky Wheel Maxim

Most people feel that complaining about poor service, shoddy merchandise, or rudeness and mistreatment is a waste of time. That doesn't stop them from doing it, though. They complain to their spouses, their friends, their relatives, even virtual strangers. But rarely do they complain to the person or persons who can do something about their problem.

Remember the old maxim: "The squeaky wheel gets the grease"? If you quietly accept your misfortune, you are certainly not going to find satisfaction. But if you complain—in the right way, to the right person, chances are someone will do something about it, if only to get you off that person's back! And the best way to complain is through a well-crafted complaint letter.

Letters of complaint are perhaps the single most effective means of getting wrongs righted, getting mistakes cleared up, or getting refunds. The letters need not be fancy or long, and you don't have to be an expert writer. Simply follow the steps outlined in this book, and you'll be writing clear, effective letters.

You may be wondering, if it's so easy, why doesn't everyone do it? The truth is, most people are under the impression that complaining will do them no good. They think that whoever receives their letter will simply toss it in the wastebasket. "Why should the company president pay attention to me?" they think.

He or she *will* pay attention to you, and for several good reasons. First of all, no one becomes president of a company by ignoring the concerns of his or her customers. At least, no one stays president for long under those circumstances. Second, few professionals offering a product or service to the public can afford too many dissatisfied customers. If enough of them become unhappy, they will go elsewhere and the business or practice will suffer. Third, if you make it clear that you are not going to give up until you are satisfied, the people you pester *have* to pay attention—and they may do what you ask just so you'll leave them alone.

The bottom line: retail and service companies have good reasons for keeping you happy and for satisfying your complaints. Word-of-mouth is a powerful tool—or weapon, depending on how it's used. Studies show that customers tell twice as many people about bad experiences as they do about good ones. This type of negative advertising can send a company's image plummeting.

Therefore, ignoring complaints, or treating them lightly, can be disastrous. One airline shuttle passenger, after enduring abysmal service and a cavalier dismissal of his complaint, wrote a scathing article, which was published in the *New York Times*. That article must have cost the airline a great deal of money—certainly many times what it would have cost to satisfy that one unhappy customer.

And addressing customer complaints (even just listening to them) can dramatically enhance company or product loyalty. When companies invest in complaint-handling departments, the return on the investment can be as much as 170%, according to a study by a Washington, D.C. consulting firm. Higher customer satisfaction means greater brand loyalty, which translates to bigger profits.

Companies like British Airways, Whirlpool, Coca-Cola, and Fidelity Investments take this kind of information and advice seriously. They have set up special departments and phone systems to handle complaints. In Coca-Cola's case, this may have saved the company an enormous amount of money. When the "New Coke" was put on the market in 1985, the company received a flood of complaint calls over its new 1-800-GET-COKE lines. The almost immediate negative customer input, and the company's quick response in releasing Coke Classic, prevented a potentially devastating financial loss.

In cases like this, phone complaints can be effective. For a specific problem, though, a letter is a more powerful way to get your message across. Phone calls can be easily forgotten once the receiver is back in the cradle. And you may not feel like pursuing the matter once you have gotten the complaint off your chest. Furthermore, words cannot be retracted when spoken. If you make the mistake of calling to complain when you are still angry or frustrated, you may say things that hurt your cause and that you may later regret.

In a letter, you can carefully weigh your words, avoiding emotional outbursts. The result will be a reasoned, logical, hard-to-dismiss appeal for fair treatment. A letter is also a permanent record that can be traced and easily copied and sent to others. It leaves a paper trail that is hard to ignore.

The Lemon

Patricia Westheimer bought an expensive sedan a few years ago, made by an automaker noted for high quality. Of course, any assembly line will produce one or two lemons. The sedan was plagued with problems from the beginning: the sunroof would stick, the radio wouldn't work, the transmission malfunctioned repeatedly, and the brakes went out more than once. The car was constantly in the shop.

Finally, Patricia became fed up with the problems. Her verbal complaints seemed to fall on deaf ears. So she wrote a clear, succinct letter to the president of the dealership, in which she documented her complaints and stated her requirements for satisfaction: she wanted (1) the best Honda on the lot (it was a dual dealership); (2) money back on the trade; and (3) never to have to drive the lemon again. A few days later the president's secretary called to arrange a meeting with the president in his office. Shortly after the meeting, Patricia drove away in a new Honda. All of her demands were met.

This is not an isolated incident. The techniques Patricia Westheimer used have worked time and time again, both for us and for many others.

In our research for this book we turned up dozens of complaint letters, some good, some not so good. But in every case, the authors of the letters had decided that they had had enough. Rather than just complain to those closest to them, they decided to take action and do something about their problem. Here are a few of their situations, and the letters they wrote that got results.

The Ineffective Attorney

After enduring an unpleasant divorce and paying several hundred dollars in alimony for over a year, Robert Morrison of Boise, Idaho discovered that his wife had been living with another man for months and had not told her ex-husband. He began withholding alimony. She initiated legal action to get it back, denying that she had another means of support. Morrison hired a law firm to fight the suit, but the service he received was substandard. Then Morrison discovered that his wages were being garnished. He wrote the following letter to the president of the law firm.

June 15, 1993
Robert Morrison
125 Canada St.
Boise, ID 87334

Mr. Marshall Daniels
Daniels, Klein, Horowitz, and Thompson
885 Central Blvd.
Boise, ID 87336

Dear Mr. Daniels:

Although my company has employed your firm in the past, with good results, I'm afraid my experience with you has been less than satisfactory. Yesterday I discovered that my wages were being garnished, and I am holding you responsible.

In January of this year I discovered that my ex-wife, to whom I have been paying alimony for almost a year, was living with another man. She was, in fact, being supported in full by this man. I let her know that I was aware of the situation and stopped alimony payments. She immediately hired an attorney (Saul Rubin), denied that she had any other support, and initiated legal action to force me to resume payments. It was at that point that I engaged your firm, in the person of Mr. Williams.

From the beginning Mr. Williams was not very helpful. He always seemed to be too busy to pay much attention to my problem. When I called your office he was often impossible to reach, and only twice in the last two months has he returned my calls. I don't know what, if anything, Mr. Williams has done on my behalf, but his efforts seemed to have had no effect on my ex-wife's harassment through Mr. Rubin. Now I find that my income is being taken from me.

Over the past two months I have paid your firm $357.95. Since I have received no discernible benefit, I wish to have that $357.95 refunded. Also, I do not believe I should suffer economic inconvenience due to faulty representation on the part of your staff. I want you to replace my lost income of $750.00, and guarantee that amount to me every month until this problem is resolved.

I am certain that, had you personally been aware of this problem, it would not have gone this far. I am confident you will do everything possible to rectify the situation.

Sincerely,

Robert Morrison

Two weeks after sending this letter, Mr. Morrison's $750.00 was recovered and his $357.95 refunded, along with a personal letter of apology from Mr. Daniels. A week later he received a bill from the law firm for $155.00, for new work done on his behalf, which he gladly paid.

The Unhappy Passenger

Who among us has not had a problem with an airline? Perhaps more than any other business or industry, a poorly run airline can make you feel like a head of livestock. Here's a case where a dissatisfied customer fought back.

September 17, 1993

Mr. Roger Bantell
Chairman of the Board
Worldwide Airlines
2373 Colorado Ave.
Denver, CO 85786

Dear Mr. Bantell:

Until recently I have been very happy with the service your airline delivers. However, this week I had a most unpleasant experience aboard one of your planes. The service was horrible. Since service is what I paid for when I bought the ticket, I would like the purchase price of the ticket, in the amount of $289.00, refunded to me.

When I boarded Worldwide Flight 21 from Denver to Buffalo on September 15, I found there was already someone sitting in my assigned seat. When I mentioned this to a flight attendant she took my boarding pass and asked me to wait near the food preparation area while she looked into it. A few moments later another flight attendant asked to see my ticket and itinerary. I didn't see why that was necessary. When I said so, this attendant became very rude and told me that I'd be lucky to get a seat at all unless I did what she said. I gave her my ticket and she left.

A few minutes later she returned and told me my seat had been changed to the smoking area at the back of the plane. I told her that I had expressly asked for a non-smoking seat, and that I was very sensitive to cigarette smoke. I asked if there wasn't anything else available, in first class perhaps. Again, she was very rude and made a point of saying very loudly that the plane could not leave the terminal until I sat down. I did so and, surrounded by smokers, had the worst flight of my life.

Mr. Bantell, I understand that the flight was filled to overflowing, and mixups do occur, but the rude treatment I received was inexcusable. Furthermore, I feel some other arrangement could have been made to spare me the nausea and discomfort I experienced in the smoking area. I'm sure you'll agree that my request for a refund is reasonable.

I look forward to hearing from you.

Sincerely,

Margaret Haines
6678 Fetler Ave.
Buffalo, NY 10234

As a result of this letter, Ms. Haines received not only a full refund on her ticket, but also a voucher for a free round-trip flight on Worldwide Airlines anywhere in the continental United States.

The Popper That Didn't Pop

Many of the letters we've seen concerned shoddy merchandise or poor workmanship. The next letter is a typical example.

January 4, 1994

Joseph Parnelli
1227 Beryl St.
San Diego, CA 92119

Kyle Allenson
Manager
K&P Department Stores
3465 Lakeview
Lakeside, CA 92029

Dear Mr. Allenson:

On December 21, 1993, I purchased a HOT-TOP hot air popcorn popper from your store. It does not work and I would like a full refund of the purchase price ($16.96 plus tax).

The popper was a Christmas gift to my daughter. When she used it for the first time on December 30, it did not work very well. Most of the popcorn was left unpopped. When we tried it again on January 1, 1994, the results were even worse. Also, on this occasion, the popper began to smoke from its motor.

When I took the popper back to your store to return it, I was told that sale items cannot be returned. This seems clearly unfair. The device never worked properly, sale item or not. I can't believe you want your customers treated this way, and I'm confident you'll see to it that the matter is cleared up.

Sincerely,

Joseph Parnelli

Mr. Parnelli received an apologetic call from Mr. Allenson, who instructed him to return the popper to the store for a full refund.

The Broken Appliance

Anyone who has ever paid rent knows that landlords can be frustrating. We often wait for weeks to have a leaking faucet repaired or an appliance replaced. The following letter is from someone who did something about it.

June 11, 1993

Betty Simmons
Manager
Oak Glen Apartments
37897 Fuerte
La Mesa, CA 92045

Dear Ms. Simmons:

As you know, I've been a resident here for almost three years. I have been satisfied with the apartment and the living arrangements—until now. In the past month I have called the maintenance department four times to have a malfunctioning refrigerator either fixed or replaced. Each time I call I am told it will be done, but it never is. I'm afraid my patience is wearing thin.

The refrigerator runs constantly but does not maintain a low temperature. So I'm enclosing a bill in the amount of $78.10 for the excess electricity the refrigerator has used and for food that spoiled. I've also reviewed the rental contract, which states that all reasonable repairs are to be completed within 30 days. That deadline has now been exceeded. My first call was placed on May 7.

I'm sure you will agree that my requests for refund and repair are reasonable. I look forward to hearing from you.

Yours,

Ellen Dahlstrom

Ms. Dahlstrom's refrigerator was replaced within two days. The manager balked at refunding the $78.10, however, so Ellen followed up with a letter to the owner. She included a copy of the first letter, and copies of all pertinent receipts. A copy of this second letter was sent to the manager:

June 18, 1993

Mr. E. K. Harris
Sun Developments
577 Galveston Blvd.
Houston, TX 73221

Dear Mr. Harris:

I have encountered a problem, which is outlined in the enclosed letter. Ms. Simmons was most helpful in seeing to it that my faulty refrigerator was promptly replaced. However, she didn't seem to feel she had the authority to reimburse me for lost food and for excess electricity. So I am sending the bill for $78.10 to you.

It does not seem reasonable to me that I should suffer financial loss due to slow or inefficient service on the part of your maintenance staff. I'm sure you'll agree. I look forward to a full reimbursement and to a continuing relationship with your company.

Sincerely,

Ellen Dahlstrom

cc: Betty Simmons

Ten days later, Ms. Dahlstrom received a check for $78.10. Tenants often feel they have little leverage over landlords. However, it can be costly to lose a tenant. Even if the apartment is rented immediately it must still be cleaned and painted, and faulty appliances must be replaced. This "downtime" with the accompanying upgrade is expensive. If you ever find yourself having a problem with a landlord, you can note these facts in a complaint letter.

The Rude Receptionist

Doctors' offices can present their own special challenge when it comes to complaint letters. The following letter illustrates one situation:

April 22, 1993

Dr. Ted Hunter
Plaza Medical Center
989 Broadway
Phoenix, AZ 88765

Dear Dr. Hunter:

For six years I have enjoyed a good relationship with you and your staff. Unfortunately,
my visit to your office last week was not in
keeping with my past experience.

As you know, I came in to try out a new pair
of contact lenses. Since your office was very
busy at the time and all of your mirrors were
in use, I went down the hallway to the bathroom to put the contacts in.

When I returned home I discovered that my
glasses were missing and realized I had left
them in the bathroom. I had an important
meeting to attend and could not come back to
your office. But when I called your receptionist and asked if she would walk down to
the bathroom and retrieve the glasses for me,
she refused. Not only that, she was very
rude. She told me that I would have to come
back and get them myself. Finally, after a
very unpleasant conversation, she put me
through to Peggy, your assistant, who kindly
agreed to go get my glasses.

I thought I should make you aware of how some
members of your staff treat your customers.
Even though everyone was very busy at the
time, rudeness has no place in any business.
I would like your assurance that something
like this will never happen again.

Sincerely,

John Williams

Mr. Williams received a personal apology from Dr. Hunter and an assurance that the experience would not be repeated.

These letters represent only a small sample of what we have seen, but they are an indication of what you can accomplish if you make your grievances known in a rational, non-emotional way. We have found that company owners, presidents, and managers are usually intelligent and reasonable people. They know that no company can survive with dissatisfied customers; if word gets out that a company or professional practice provides poor service, its reputation often suffers irreparable damage. Company executives also know that spending a few dollars now to satisfy your complaint will probably make you a loyal customer for life—which translates to a return of many times on their investment.

Throughout the rest of this book we'll provide more examples of complaint letters that got results—and a few that didn't. We'll show you what works and what doesn't, and we'll help you gain the skills and confidence necessary to write a powerful, effective complaint letter.

When to Commit Your Gripe to Paper

Should you sit down and write a letter every time something goes wrong? Should you complain every time someone is rude to you, and every time you are unhappy with a service or product? Probably not. Most of us are far too busy to devote the kind of time that would take—and crafting an effective, well-written letter does take time. If your problem can be solved with a quick phone call or another visit to the store or service center, we recommend you take that route.

A woman we know recently had the brakes on her car fixed. Two days after the repair, the brakes went out of adjustment. She drove the car back to the repair shop where the shop foreman dropped what he was doing and immediately fixed the problem. Courteous customer service is not dead! Whether the foreman's action was true courtesy or enlightened self-interest doesn't matter. His actions guaranteed that our friend will always take her car to him for service.

In this instance a letter of complaint would obviously have been inappropriate. On the other hand, if the foreman had refused to guarantee his work, a letter to his boss would have been in order.

Another acquaintance of ours purchased a videotape recorder, which did not work properly. She took it back to the store and insisted on a replacement. Though it had been a sale item, the store manager approved the transaction. Many stores have good complaint/return departments and are willing to do what is necessary to keep their customers happy. Keeping customers satisfied, after all, is simply good business.

In another case, Al Sestendona purchased a non-spilling coffee mug to use in his car. Unfortunately, the mug did not live up to its claim. When Al took it back for a refund he was told there was nothing wrong with the mug. Since it was not obviously defective, the clerk would not give Al a refund. The clerk merely suggested that Mr. Sestendona be more careful. No matter how much Al protested, he was refused. Finally, he gave up, threw the mug in the wastebasket, and stormed out of the store. Though a letter of complaint would have been quite appropriate, Mr. Sestendona simply registered his displeasure by never shopping in that store again.

In this case, the principle of "return on investment" applies. It simply was not worth Mr. Sestendona's time to find out the name of the convenience chain owner or the manufacturer and write a letter to recover his lost $2.89. The effort was more trouble than the mug was worth.

Sometimes, too, a quick phone call can solve your problem. As we described in the last chapter, many corporations maintain complaint departments specifically designed to deal with problems. Jim Mastro applied for and received a new credit card, but found that his name had been misspelled. He made a call to the bank's service department and had a new card, with the name correctly spelled, within a week.

ADVANTAGES OF THE LETTER

Generally, if your problem is simple and a phone call will solve it, we recommend taking that route. Sometimes, however, a phone call won't do the job. Getting through to the person who has the power to do something about your problem can be almost impossible, especially with large companies that have not instituted customer service or complaint departments. Presidents and chairpersons of the board rarely pick up their own phones, which means you are forced to deal with a secretary or receptionist first. Secretaries can wield enormous power. If they refuse to put your call through, or if the president is always "in a meeting" or "out of the office," you can do very little about it.

So our advice is this: When there is a significant amount of money involved, or your phone calls go unanswered, or you are simply frustrated and fed up with rotten service, it's time to write a letter.

In these cases, a letter has many advantages over a phone call. Phone calls are easy to forget. There is no record of them. When you finally get through to the person you are trying to reach, if you ever do, he or she can simply claim ignorance of any message that you called. And once you hang up the receiver, your words can be easily ignored.

A letter, on the other hand, is permanent. Writing creates a paper trail. If you finally get in touch with the person you are trying to reach on the phone, and he or she claims your letter was never received, or it was misplaced, you can always send him or her a copy. Letters can't dissipate into the air like spoken words.

Sometimes, too, it's difficult to organize your thoughts and get across in a brief phone call everything you have to say. It's often easy to forget one or two important points or arguments, even if you have them written down in front of you. And you are not always in control of the conversation.

When writing a letter, you can take all the time you need and carefully organize your thoughts and arguments for maximum impact. You can include all the facts and figures you need to document your case, including copies of receipts or correspondence to support your argument. Because of their permanence, letters carry more weight than phone calls. Whereas phone calls can be ignored, people often feel compelled to deal with letters. *In most cases a letter is the single most powerful and effective means you have at your disposal for registering a complaint.*

The Wine Glass Episode

A few years ago, a large department store sent Jim Mastro a set of four inscribed wine glass that he had never requested. He sent them back almost immediately but was billed for the items nonetheless. He called several times to try to clear the matter up but was given the "phone run-around" each time. The store claimed the returned merchandise had never been received by the subcontractor who manufactured it. When Jim received his next bill, not only was the item still listed, but so too was a finance charge on the unpaid balance. Finally, he wrote this letter to the credit department:

Martha Pendaker
Jobber's Emporium
3465 Lakeview
Milwaukee, WI 54893

RE: Acct. # 2874635, Transaction # 88985-9

Dear Ms. Pendaker:

As I'm sure you know, I've been trying to clear up this matter of missing wine glasses for over a month. To sum up, on about April 14 I requested the free sample advertised in your mailer. I received the sample on May 3 but declined any further shipments, as instructed. Nonetheless, on May 24 I received a shipment of four additional glasses and was billed $88.95.

I returned the glasses and the unpaid bill to the shipper, Engraving Designs, Inc., in Huntsville, AL, on May 25. Though I made the mistake of not sending them via registered mail, I have enclosed a photocopy of the postal receipt in the amount of $4.40.

Now Engraving Designs claims they never received the package with the glasses. My suspicion is that, when they noticed with glee that the package was not registered, they simply tossed it into the dumpster. With no record of the package's receipt, they could then be spared the cost of the glasses and the engraving. Once they were engraved with my name, of course, the glasses were useless to anyone but me and could not be re-used.

I suggest you look into this possibility. For now, I will not pay for items that I did not accept and do not have. I would like you to credit my account for $93.35, which is the cost of the glasses themselves and the postage I paid to ship them back.

I have been a steady customer of Jobber's for many years, as my credit record will testify. I intend to continue the relationship as long as this annoying little matter can be satisfactorily cleared up.

Thank you,

Sincerely,

Jim Mastro

This letter contains more sarcasm than we would generally recommend. However, the author's account was credited with the desired amount. In essence, this letter, along with the accompanying documentation, did more to solve the problem than several phone calls.

The Benefit Plan

Here's another instance where a letter got results after several phone calls did not:

September 2, 1993

Mainline Auto Injection
3399 Main St.
Los Angeles, CA 90445

RE: Defined Benefit Pension Plan / Defined Contribution Money Purchase Pension Plan

Dear Mr. Hathaway:

On behalf of the shop employees, I am writing to you in reference to the above captioned Defined Benefit Pension Plan and/or the Defined Contribution Money Purchase Pension Plan.

We know that as participants in the Company's Retirement Plan, we are entitled to obtain the following information and are hereby giving you official written request for that information:

• Copy of all plan documents and other plan information;
• A summary of the plan's annual financial report;
• A statement telling whether we have a right to receive a pension at retirement age, and if so, what the benefits would be at retirement age if we stopped working for the company now.

Your cooperation and prompt attention to this matter will be greatly appreciated.

Sincerely,

John Dunbar
Shop Foreman

Although Mr. Hathaway had put off Mr. Dunbar's phone calls for weeks, this letter got the desired results. Apparently, having the letter in front of him seemed to make the matter more "official" for Mr. Hathaway.

THE PHONE CALL FOLLOW-UP

We should reiterate at this point that phone calls do have a place in the complaint process, even in cases where your first recourse is to write a letter. It is sometimes a good idea to follow up your letter with a phone call. Once your name has been seen by company officials, in the form of a well-organized, reasoned argument, they are frequently more willing to respond favorably to a phone call. If you're in a hurry, this technique can speed up the response to your complaint. Send the letter, wait about 10 days, and then call. Chances are good that your phone call will be routed to the appropriate person.

Following up letters with phone calls is a good strategy for another reason: it keeps your name in front of the offending party or organization. This can be vital. If your name keeps popping up—on letters and phone messages—every time the boss turns around, he or she will be unlikely to forget you or procrastinate when dealing with your complaint.

The Write-Call-Write Sequence

We recommend the write-call-write sequence if your first letter or phone call doesn't get the desired response. As noted previously, write the first letter, wait 10 days, and then call. If you still can't get through, write a second letter using a stronger tone. State your complaint and demands again, briefly, and enclose a copy of the first letter. This may also be the time to begin sending copies out to the appropriate agencies. (See Chapter 3 and Chapter 9 for more about "cc's" and stronger letters.)

The write-call-write sequence can and should also be used

when your complaint is satisfactorily addressed. Here's an example:

Patricia Westheimer travels extensively and is a member of a prestigious airline executive club. Recently, however, she was 300 miles short of the mileage required for renewal, and the airline was threatening to cancel her "exclusive flyer" membership. She wrote to the airline's president, noting that she was a valuable, steady customer and that she would be in Europe at the cut-off time (and therefore unable to complete the mileage on time), but that within a week of the cut-off she would be flying home on the airline.

A few days later, Patricia called the president's office and spoke to his secretary, who remembered seeing the letter. The secretary promised to call back—and did, with the news that the executive club membership would be extended. Patricia immediately wrote a second letter, thanking the president and his secretary for their help and understanding.

In this case, the second letter was used as a courtesy. In extending this courtesy, her original complaint became a stepping-stone to building a stronger and more positive relationship with the company.

We feel this is a wise thing to do in any situation where a complaint is satisfactorily addressed. Patricia's "thank-you" letter almost guarantees that she'll be remembered positively. If she ever has another grievance with this airline, she's confident that it will be dealt with promptly.

Follow-up phone calls, of course, may not always be appropriate. There are times when it is simply impossible to get through to anyone. But when phone calls *are* an option, they can be used to establish personal communication with the offending party. By giving him or her the opportunity to associate a voice and personality with your letter, you become more real, more human. In this busy, impersonal world we live in, that extra effort can give you a crucial edge.

A final note on secretaries is in order here. As we said before, secretaries wield enormous power. They often control who gets through to the president or chairperson, and when. It's worth whatever effort it takes for you to get the secretary on your side. When you speak to him or her, be courteous and cheerful. Remember: he or she is a critical bridge between you and the person to whom you want to speak. Never, but NEVER, get angry at the secretary. Whatever has happened to you, it is almost certainly not the secretary's fault. And, as the above story illustrates, the secretary can play an important part in reaching the solution you desire.

THE FIRST LETTER

Let's say you have tried phone calls and they have gotten you nowhere. When you call you get busy signals, and when you finally do get through you get the run-around. So you've decided to write a letter. What now?

The first thing you must do is decide what you want your letter to accomplish. What is the letter's purpose? Do you just want to let off steam? Do you want to point out an unpleasant situation, with the hope that something will be done about it? Or do you have a specific complaint and a specific solution in mind?

All three reasons for writing a complaint letter are valid, but you must decide on yours before you start writing. This decision will determine what you say and how you go about saying it. If you wish only to get something off your chest, you can adopt a stronger tone immediately. After all, you're not trying to get someone on your side; your purpose is simply to make yourself feel better.

Take a look at the following example:

June 22, 1993

Barry Kein
Executive President
Ohio Seventh Savings
4588 Central Pkwy
Toledo, OH 34221

Dear Mr. Kein:

I've been using your bank for about a year now, but that is about to come to an end. The service has never been good. Yesterday it was rotten. Really rotten.

I had 45 minutes for lunch, as I usually do. I spent half of it waiting in line at your bank. There were only two tellers on duty, while the rest stood around and chatted with each other. At this time there was a line of almost 20 people. When I asked what was going on, I was informed they were on their lunch break.

I expressed my dissatisfaction to my teller when I finally reached the window. She suggested I try another bank "if I didn't like it." Well, that's exactly what I'm doing. Consider my account canceled. I've got a good mind to report you clowns to the federal government!

You call your place of business a bank. I call it a circus!

Disgustedly,

Raymond Wilson
1223 Hathaway Place
Toledo, OH 34332

Mr. Wilson made no attempt to obtain an apology or any kind of restitution. Nor was he interested in effecting a change in bank policy, since he had already canceled his account. He wanted only to let the bank president know how angry he was. And, in that respect, he certainly succeeded. The strong tone of the letter made his feelings quite clear. But, by the same token, that tone did nothing to solve the problem or develop a constructive relationship with the bank president. Mr. Kein probably tossed it into the nearest trash receptacle. After all, why try reasoning with someone as angry as that, someone who had already taken his money elsewhere?

This point is worth remembering. If you need to express your anger and don't care about "burning a bridge," then write a letter like this. Bear in mind, however, if Mr. Wilson ever needs anything from this bank, such as a credit reference, he is probably not going to get it.

Be Constructive

You can express anger or dissatisfaction without resorting to insults and threats. If you adopt a reasonable, businesslike tone you may be able to effect a change in the way a company operates, even if you don't ask for anything specific.

For instance, let's say you've finally managed to straighten out your electric bill, but you had to deal with a curt and rude utility representative while doing so:

July 9, 1993

Office of Consumer Affairs
General Gas and Electric Co.
677 Watt St.
San Jose, CA 93228

On the above date I called your Fresno office to inquire about two situations. One, I had been without my phone-answering service for three days due to a power shut-off in the office below mine. Obviously, my phone-answering system used electricity from the office below. I was told that it would be back on the following Monday, but by this morning it had not been restored.

Second, I had received my billing for my home address without reference to the cost per kwh anywhere on the invoice. Since we had not used more electricity in my home, but the bill had jumped by $40 or so, I simply wanted to know how much more I was being charged in June than in May per kwh.

The service representative I spoke with was beyond rude and insulting. He offered his name only as "Gary" and snidely stated that he didn't have to give out any more information than that.

He blatantly told me that (a) I was stupid and didn't know how to read a utility bill, that (b) it wasn't his problem that my phones didn't work, and (c) he didn't have a clue when I might expect to have power.

This rude and cavalier attitude is reprehensible. If I were dealing with a company that had competition in the market-place, this simply would not happen. I would like your assur-ance that it will not happen again.

Very sincerely,

Ken Holmes
President
Chandler Communications

cc: Public Utilities Commission
Office of Consumer Affairs/FEA
GG&E Fresno

Though Mr. Holmes wanted nothing more than to voice a gripe, he wisely avoided blaming anyone other than the person directly responsible, "Gary." His letter is written in a style that invites a response by the electric company higher-ups. That is a point to remember: Even if all you want is to make your anger known, it is always a good idea to be reasonable. After all, why insult the very people who can do something about your complaint?

Also, it is always important to state the circumstances of your complaint clearly. Random, generalized complaints carry little weight. Be specific. If the top executive you address can see all the gruesome details of your problem, the weight of the truth may inspire him or her to take action on your behalf. At the very least, a fully detailed account gives your complaint a great deal of legitimacy. For example, compare a brief letter that merely states that "service has been lousy" with the following letter:

February 18, 1994

Mr. Jake Galagos
President, Southern Cable
5593 Hurt Ct.
San Clemente, CA 91884

Dear Mr. Galagos:

I would like to relate my experience with your company.

1. Early in 1993 I phoned Southern to order cable service. I was told by the service representative that she could not find my address in the computer and she did not know why. She would look into the situation and call me back. My call was NEVER RETURNED.

2. Early in December 1993, I phoned again to order cable service. Once again the service representative told me that she could not find my address in the computer and she did not know why. She said she would look into it and call me back. I told her about my previous experience and she assured me that my call would be returned. IT WASN'T.

3. On January 18, 1994, I phoned Southern and asked for the administrative offices. The operator would not put me through to administration, stating that she needed to know the reason for the call. I explained the above, and she put my call through to Robert Jones (498-3322 x55). Mr. Jones was EXTREMELY HELPFUL. My call was returned by Margaret who scheduled an appointment for hook-up. I explained to Margaret that I would not be at home and that my neighbor would take care of everything. She said he could sign for me on the work order and he could give my check to the installer.

4. I had the electrician install a cable as Margaret directed.

5. My neighbor stayed home from 12-5 as indicated on the card (copy enclosed). Southern never showed!

6. I called and was given the run-around. I was told that Janet, the supervisor, would call me.

7. I called Janet the next day. She also gave me the run-around and insisted that it was my fault! She said the installer tried to call my home. I had told Margaret I would not be there. The answering machine was on and no message was left. Janet also said the installer had tried to call my office number. I was not called at my office. I work in a physician's office and the line does not go unanswered! Southern did not call my office! Janet insisted they did, and she was not helpful.

Please note the instructions on the card your office mailed to me.

As it is, I am out the money I paid to install the cable you required. If I had this much trouble just trying to get service, I am very dubious about what kind of service your company would deliver. Over the weekend I inquired about your service and I did not hear good things. Therefore, I called this morning, spoke to Anne, and canceled my order for cable.

I am disappointed that we will not be able to see the Arts & Entertainment Network, the Discovery Channel, etc., and am upset that I am out the cable hook-up fee, but as you can see I do not have confidence in your company.

Sincerely,

Mindy Hansen
4455 Ocean Drive
San Clemente, CA 91443

Though Ms. Hansen made no specific requests and was essentially just letting off steam, this letter resulted in (1) a definite appointment so she wouldn't have to wait all day, (2) free hook-up, and (3) free service for three months. A clear, concise, well-documented letter like this can often compel the company president to take action.

A Little Sarcasm

The tone in these last two letters is fairly strong. When you're not asking for anything, you can be almost as blunt as you want, although, as we said earlier, it is better to be reasonable and businesslike than insulting. Besides, a rude and nasty letter doesn't do anyone any good, and you may later feel foolish for sending it.

Still, there may be times when a little biting sarcasm is in order. See, for example, the next letter.

Mrs. Sally Kahn
886 Central Hwy.
Del Mar, CA 92035
May 24, 1993

Goodstuff Foods Co.
599 South Mall
San Jose, CA 94667

Dear Sirs:

The bug you see—enclosed herein—is now dead. But it was alive inside my package of Goodstuff cornbread stuffing. It was flying around inside the plastic bag . . . I cut the bag open . . . it flew out . . .
I killed it.
Disgusting.
Of course, I threw out the entire box. But the question is bigger than a bread crumb box: What kind of quality control do you have?
Are your products carrying disease-bearing critters?
I would hope you look into this very seriously.

Very truly yours,

Sally Kahn
cc: Food and Drug Administration
Washington, D.C.

You have probably noticed that both Sally Kahn and Mr. Holmes wasted no time in bringing out the big guns; both authors sent copies to appropriate agencies. When you are not expecting a refund, a free ticket, or some other form of remuneration and you just want to let off steam—blast away! Sending out copies in this manner is designed to hit your target hard, give the readers the jitters, and make them pay for the inconvenience they have caused you.

Also, if you are in an exceptionally big hurry to straighten out a problem, it will probably speed things up considerably if you send out copies right away.

The drawback to going this route is that if your letter doesn't get results, you may not have very many options left. So if you are trying to get your money back from a recalcitrant company, we recommend holding off on the copies until they are absolutely necessary.

Copies are like trump cards: you don't want to play them all at once if your objective is to win the game. We'll talk more about sending copies in Chapter 3.

Getting a Positive Result

What if you want to let off steam, like Sally Kahn, Mindy Hansen, and Ken Holmes above, and also want to see something specific done about the situation that caused your anger?

Compare the following letter with Mr. Wilson's nasty one earlier in this chapter.

November 19, 1993

Dorothy Edwards
Manager
Central Coast Bank
547 Coast Blvd.
Monterey, CA 95043

Dear Ms. Edwards:

I'm afraid I had a rather unpleasant experience in your bank the other day. At my job, I have only 30 minutes for lunch. This gives me only a limited amount of time to complete any banking business I may have that cannot be accomplished via automatic teller.

On November 17 I went to your bank at 12:00 to transfer some funds and withdraw cash. I waited in line for 20 minutes before I finally got up to the teller! During this time there were only three tellers on duty, yet there were others around who seemed to be on break or off duty. They made no effort to ease the crunch. Further, when I complained to my teller, she was rather curt.

Ms. Edwards, I have been a customer here for over a year. I'd prefer not to change banks unless it is absolutely necessary. I wonder if there might not be some other way the bank could arrange breaks so that the busiest times are better covered by your staff. Also, busy or not, rudeness is never good business.

I appreciate your attention to this matter.

Sincerely,

Lisa Johnson
8789 Hillside
Monterey, CA 95045

Ms. Johnson received this reply:

November 23, 1993

Dorothy Edwards
Manager
Central Coast Bank
547 Coast Blvd.
Monterey, CA 95043

Lisa Johnson
8789 Hillside
Monterey, CA 95045

Dear Ms. Johnson:
Please accept my sincere apologies for the treatment
you received on November 17 and for the delay in
service. Unfortunately, even the best system falls
apart occasionally, and that was the case on Wednes-
day.

However, your suggestion is well taken, and we have
begun a review of scheduling and breaks. I expect
some changes will be made. I assure you that your
experience will not be repeated.

If you have any other problems or suggestions,
please contact me.

Sincerely,

Dorothy Edwards
Manager

Ms. Johnson's letter had a dual purpose: to let off steam *and* get something done about her problem. Complaining for its own sake, though it may make you feel better, is not very useful. There may be times, of course, when there really is nothing that can be done about your gripe, in which case it is better to express your anger and frustration than hold it in.

However, we have found that in almost every case where there is a valid complaint, some reparative action can be taken. If you are going to go to the trouble of writing a complaint letter, use the opportunity to effect some change in the offending system, or obtain redress, or both.

That is the essence of an effective complaint letter—one that gets results.

The Unfriendly Detergent Cap

January 31, 1994

Single & Dribe
Consumer Services
P.O. Box 669
Cleveland, OH 45221

RE: Lemon Spritzer Detergent

Recently I purchased your Lemon Spritzer Liquid Automatic Dishwashing Detergent for two reasons:

1. I had used your dry dishwasher detergent in the past and was impressed with its performance and was anxious to try the liquid version.
2. Your brand was one of the lowest-priced liquid detergents on the shelf and I am a cost-conscious shopper.

However, when using the detergent at home, I found the protective cap extremely difficult to remove. After using the product several times, I came to the conclusion that paying more for another brand might be preferable to struggling with the cap each time.

If you pay any attention to consumer input, please consider redoing the cap on this product. You will have my business back because I really do like your liquid detergent and its price.

Thank you for listening.

Sincerely,

Mrs. Linda Youngston
9864 Spring Road
San Diego, CA 92129

Indeed, like any good company, Single & Dribe does listen to consumer input. Mrs. Youngston received a letter from the director of consumer services, who apologized for the problem and informed Mrs. Youngston that a new cap was being engineered. Included in the envelope was a coupon for two free bottles of detergent.

Mopping Up on a Complaint

January 10, 1994

16 Medora Dr.
Bismarck, ND 58502
(701) 256-0012

EasyMop Manufacturing Co.
P.O. Box 1819
Owings Mills, NJ 08055

Dear Sirs:

You say you offer a full FIVE YEAR WARRANTY? How about a 5-day warranty!

This mop fell apart immediately. You can see I still had your cardboard promotional packaging, as enclosed.

But not $10.89.

My oh my. Even at less than $5 this is a dreadfully inferior product. I had always bought Clean-Rite products, but your squeezer gizmo looked intriguing, and I thought I'd try it.

Well, dear sirs, I would like you to send me my $10.89. I won't even hold you responsible for the sales tax!

I will be looking forward to my check. Thank you.

Very truly yours,

Janet Kendall

Mrs. Kendall received a very apologetic phone call from the president's secretary, a letter containing a check for $10.89, and, a few days later, a new mop via UPS. The new mop performed perfectly.

Both letters asked for and got results. And that, we feel, is the essence of an effective complaint letter. Letting off steam is great for the psyche, but receiving a free travel voucher or a full refund in response to a complaint makes complaining seem more worth while. Our opinion: Whenever possible, ask for what you deserve. When you've been wronged, pick up your pen or turn on your word processor and write! Remember, though, you can achieve results without using sarcasm or bitterness.

Throughout the rest of this book, we will emphasize just the type of complaint letter that asks for—and gets—specific action. The first point we'll cover is perhaps the most important: To whom do you write to register a complaint? The answer is simpler than you might think.

Whom to Complain to: Or, Whom *Does* It Concern?

If a sales clerk is unforgivably rude to you, writing a complaint letter to that person is not likely to get you an apology, nor is it likely to alter the way that business operates. If another clerk sells you faulty merchandise and then refuses to exchange it or refund your money, writing a letter to the clerk will probably not result in your money being returned. Even if you write to the manager of the store, he or she may opt to toss your letter in the trash bin. After all, why should anyone show an incriminating letter to his or her boss? No one wants to look bad, especially when one's job could be at risk.

As far as egos, reputations, and job securities go, it's safer and easier for the clerk or lower-level manager to stall and hope the writer will just forget about the problem—or at least not be willing to expend any more effort on it.

If, on the other hand, you address your letter to the president of the corporation, the regional manager of the department store chain, or the owner of the company, your letter carries more impact. You are much more likely to get a positive response and satisfaction from your complaint.

Owners and presidents have a lot more at stake; they have much more to lose by ignoring your complaint. It's *their* company and their reputation, both personally and professionally. Where the managers and clerks are just doing a job,

owners, presidents, and chairpersons of the board have often invested their lives and fortunes in their companies.

Also, clerks and managers often have less authority and little latitude of action. Usually they simply do not have the power to meet your demands. Owners and top executives, however, are in positions to do whatever it takes to solve a problem. We doubt that Ms. Haines (see Chapter 1) would have received a free travel voucher if she had merely written to the customer service representative at her local airport. Nor would Ms. Dahlstrom (also in Chapter 1) have received her $78.10 reimbursement for spoiled food if she had not gone further than the apartment manager.

Even if the owner or executive doesn't handle your complaint personally, letters handed down from the top are likely to receive much more attention and action than letters going the other way.

WRITE TO THE TOP

Write to the top: That's the rule. Find out the name of the person in the best position to solve your problem. Usually that's the owner or president or chairperson of the board. Address your letter directly to him or her. You can also multiply the power of your complaint by sending the same letter to both the president of a company and the local manager(s) directly responsible for your issue. By doing this you are, in effect, lighting a fire under those local managers. If they act swiftly and decisively, they look good to the higher-ups. (Or at least they don't look as bad, if the problem was their fault in the first place!) This is another way to speed things up in your favor.

A friend of ours used this very technique to solve an automatic washer problem:

May 12, 1993

Mrs. Karen Doyle
643 Milston Rd.
Boise, ID 88564

Mr. Harry Jones
Clean-Rite Corp.
1922 Lakeview Dr.
Glen Lake, IL 66034

Dear Mr. Jones:

Last month, on April 3, I purchased a Clean-Rite Model 44-R automatic clothes washer. It has never worked properly. I would like an exchange or a full refund of my $349.99.

Let me explain. I was fascinated by the new electronic features your company has introduced, particularly the light touch controls. However, since I purchased the machine, it has worked properly only twice. Several times it has stopped in mid-cycle, and I have been forced to start the load from the beginning. Sometimes the "light touch" buttons fail to respond.

When I tried to get a refund or trade on this "lemon" at Brighton's Department Store, where I bought it, I was told first by the clerk, and then by the manager, that they were not authorized to do that—even though the machine comes with a two-year warranty. Mr. Leone, the manager of Brighton's, went so far as to insult me by suggesting I wasn't using the machine properly.

Mr. Jones, let me assure you that I am capable of reading and following instructions! Frankly, I'm fed up with the run-around I'm getting. Do you or do you not guarantee your products? And if you do not, why do you sell them?

I understand that mistakes can happen on a production line. I am willing to try another machine because I really do like what you promise. Or I will settle for a full refund—your choice. But I won't settle for less.

Thank you for your attention to this matter. I look forward to hearing from you soon.

Sincerely,

Karen Doyle
cc: Ira Rosenberg, Executive President
Brighton's Department Stores
George Leone, Manager
Brighton's Glen Lake

Mrs. Doyle got her replacement washing machine, and promptly. It was delivered free of charge, and both Mr. Jones and Mr. Rosenberg called her to make sure it was working as she expected.

While several days of bickering with Mr. Leone got her nothing but insults, one brief letter to the right person got her the action she had demanded from the beginning—and the personal attention of two company presidents.

Write to the top! And spend the time and effort to find out the name of the top person.

The Importance of Names

People sometimes ask us why names are so important. What's wrong with simply writing to the consumer service center, or the office of the president? After all, letters addressed in this manner often produce results, as examples in the last chapter demonstrated. What's so important about names?

The answer is this: Generic letters are simply not as powerful as letters addressed to specific individuals. A direct, personal letter carries far more impact than an impersonal one. Consider your own experience: How do you react to letters addressed to "Occupant" or "Resident"? If you're like most people, you toss them directly into the trash!

The phrase "To Whom It May Concern" is particularly annoying. We feel if the letter concerns some random, nameless individual, it must not be intended for us! Names are important to people.

Company presidents and CEOs are no different. Letters addressed "To Whom It May Concern" are too easy to shuffle off to someone else. If anyone does read your nameless letter, it will probably be a secretary, who may or may not have the power to do anything about it. In any event, it will be up to that secretary to bring it to the attention of the boss, and he or she may have more important things to think about.

Remember, if your letter isn't directed to a specific person, no one need take responsibility for addressing your complaint.

Therefore, it is extremely important to find out the name of the person you need. The work involved in doing so is usually minimal, and the benefits far exceed the work.

Now that we've established the importance of writing to specific people, the question everyone asks is "How do you find out the name of that person?"

Finding the Name You Need

Obviously, the clerks or managers giving you grief are not likely to offer the names of their superiors. You can ask, and sometimes they will surprise you by giving you the information you desire. Often, however, they are reluctant or uncooperative. Why should they hang themselves by giving you their supervisors' names? There are other ways.

The first thing to do is check company correspondence and literature. Sometimes the catalog or instruction booklet will have a message from the president, with a picture and a name. Even if this isn't the case, such literature will almost always list a home office address.

If you can't find an address or phone number this way, it's time to use the phone. When you get home, call back to the store and ask the operator to give you the address or phone number of corporate headquarters. In most cases they will supply you with the information you request without question. If they do ask why you want it, just tell them you want to write to the company. We've never had a problem getting information this way. Once you have the phone number, it's a simple matter to call corporate headquarters and ask for the address, and the name of the president or chief executive officer (CEO). The operators or receptionists you speak to will usually be happy to oblige. If they balk at giving out names, however, you can say you are compiling a directory of businesses and CEOs for your local government, to promote corporate investment in the community or something along those lines.

If you have an address but no phone number, simply call directory assistance for that town (area code-555-1212) and request the number. Then you need only uncover the name of the person you are going to write to. (Your own phone book will contain a list of area codes for cities across the country. If the city you are seeking is not listed, a long distance operator can help you.)

Your options certainly don't end there. There's more than one way to gain access to a company president! The reference section of your own local library is a wealth of information. Several firms publish directories of American companies and corporations. These directories list the name of the company or corporation, the address, phone number, and the names of key officers. Companies are listed both alphabetically *and* by product type.

One such directory is *Standard & Poor's Register of Corporations, Directors, and Executives.* It is published by Standard & Poor's Corporation in New York and lists over 50,000 corporations. This directory comes in three volumes: corporate listings, directors and executives, and an index. The index has three parts: a listing by type of business, a geographic index, and a corporate family index which identifies subsidiaries, divisions, and affiliates.

This type of index information is fairly standard for these directories. The *Million Dollar Directory,* published by Dun's Marketing Services, Inc., contains the same data for the top 50,000 corporations in the United States.

You may also find the information you need in the *Directory of Corporate Affiliations,* published by the National Register Publishing Company. This directory also contains a geographical index, with companies listed by state and city.

The Thomas Publishing Co. publishes a reference guide called the *Thomas Register of American Manufacturers,* which lists every product and service company in the United States, large and small. The listing includes a company profile, address, phone number, a description of what that company manufactures, and the names of company officials.

If you're not sure who manufactured the item that is causing you trouble, Thomas also publishes a 12-volume compendium of services and manufactured items, alphabetically listed, with the names and addresses of the companies involved. This set is called the *Thomas Register Catalog File.*

Each state may have its own directory. In California, Database Publishing Company publishes the *California Business Register,* which contains complete information on 42,000 California companies. Check with your reference librarian to see if there is a similar directory for your state.

If the company you need information on is based in Canada, check the *Canadian Trade Index,* published by the Canadian Manufacturers' Association. This directory contains the same data as its American counterparts, but for Canadian companies only.

A word of caution: double-check with a quick phone call any name you pull out of one of these directories. Nothing elaborate is required. Just a simple "Is John Doe still the president?" will do, and we highly recommend such a step. Though each of these directories is updated on a regular basis, things can change quickly. It can be very embarrassing to write a scathing complaint letter to someone who has retired or been fired!

Also, make certain that you get the correct full name, spelling, and job title of the person to whom you are writing.

If you have any trouble locating these references, or in pulling the necessary information out of them, your local librarian can be of great assistance. We've always found them to be extremely helpful. They seem to like nothing better than a reference challenge.

What if your problem is due to a local company, service organization, or professional that is not listed in any directory? Again, an employee will usually be willing to tell you the name of the owner. However, it is easy to imagine a situation where employees are reluctant to help you complain about something they've done. Or, the owner or manager may have instructed them specifically not to hand out any information. What now?

You have at your disposal several ways of obtaining information. If you can't wrest the name of the owner from his or her employees, your next stop should be local agencies. The Chamber of Commerce in your city or town will maintain a list of companies and their owners. A quick phone call may give you exactly what you need. You can also contact the Better Business Bureau for information on local companies, although in our experience this has not been very fruitful. In fact, though we have tried several times, we have never been able to get through to the bureau where we live. You may have better luck. (See Appendix B for a list of Better Business Bureaus.)

There are other options as well. Several businesses, such as auto repair shops, law offices, and insurance companies, must be licensed by the state in which they operate. These licensing agencies can be found in your telephone directory. A quick phone call to the appropriate agency will probably get you the information you need—especially if you indicate that you are having a problem.

Also, the state tax board will have all pertinent information. If you are really having trouble locating the name of the owner, or if the company you're having a problem with is new and is not listed anywhere yet, the tax board may be able to help. In California this agency is called the State Board of Equalization. Though they are not usually in the business of giving out information, if you tell them you are having a problem and need to write a complaint letter to the owner, they may accommodate you.

When companies start up, they must register with the state board and obtain a certificate. Information contained on this certificate is public record. In fact, the company or corporation is often required to have it conspicuously posted at the place of business. That's another way to learn the name of the owner.

Knowing about these various government agencies is important for another reason: If your complaint is not addressed to your satisfaction, these agencies will become important components of your "cc" list. Often a second letter to the offending individual or organization with a list of "cc'd" government agencies at the bottom will lubricate the wheels of action.

The Unfixed Car

A friend of ours, an advertising professional, had trouble once with an auto body repair shop. The work was shoddy and the shop manager would not do anything about it. When our friend asked for the name of the owner, he was refused. A quick call to his local Chamber of Commerce got him the name he needed. Then he wrote the following letter.

June 10, 1993

Samuel Fischer
Q&E Auto Body
1854 Jansen Road
Lakeside, CA 92116

Dear Mr. Fischer:

I am not at all satisfied with the work your shop has done on my car. The paint job is uneven and does not completely mask the car's former color. The dent from my accident is still noticeable. I would like you to redo the work or else refund my $469.95 so that I can go to another shop.

Your shop manager, Jim Parskilne, has not been at all helpful in this regard. He has refused to consider finishing the job he started, and he even refused to give me your name. I can't believe this is how you want to do business.

Mr. Fischer, your shop's advertising promises satisfaction. I would hope that you would be willing to live up to that promise. I look forward to hearing from you.

Sincerely,

Alan Condit

Though this was a reasonable, well-written letter, Alan received no response. When he called 10 days later, he was refused access to Mr. Fischer. So he drafted a stronger letter and sent copies of both letters to the appropriate agencies.

June 22, 1993

Samuel Fischer
Q&E Auto Body
1854 Jansen Road
Lakeside, CA 92116

Mr. Fischer:

I am dismayed by your lack of concern for the shabby treatment I have received from your staff, and for the unacceptably substandard work they performed on my car. I have paid you a fair price for a service that, so far, has not been performed.

I'm sure I don't need to remind you that a service organization like yours survives on a satisfied clientele. On the other hand, dissatisfied customers, with reasonable and fully documented complaints, can have a serious, negative impact on business.

I urge you to take action to ensure that I am treated fairly and that my complaint is adequately addressed.

Sincerely,

Alan Condit

Enclosures: Previous correspondence

cc: San Diego Chamber of Commerce
Better Business Bureau State Licensing Board
National Association of Auto Repair Shops
San Diego County District Attorney

In his second letter to Mr. Fischer, Alan Condit made it very clear that he was not playing games. He was not going to give up until he was satisfied. It had the desired effect. Alan received a call from Fischer, who apologized and promised that the job would be redone to Alan's satisfaction. And it was.

"CC'S" AND THE PAPER TRAIL

By sending out copies, or "cc's," in this manner, you enlarge the issue considerably. This term was first devised to refer to "carbon copies." Now it can refer to any additional print or photocopy you send. You extend the "paper trail" and make other people aware of your problem. In some cases these other people or organizations may even consider themselves accountable to a degree. Trade associations, such as the National Association of Auto Repair Shops listed in Condit's letter, have a stake in keeping their image clean. They will take action to censure or penalize unscrupulous members if necessary.

Copies make it harder for the offending party to hide the problem or to ignore it. Once other people start receiving your correspondence, the scope of your complaint expands. The offending party can usually see that he or she is better off taking care of the situation before the problem gets any larger.

And larger it can get. Though Alan hit hard in his second letter, he by no means exhausted his reserve of heavy weapons. If a third letter had been necessary, he likely would have included the state attorney general, a legal firm, and local consumer advocates on the list of "cc's."

For your part, it takes only a little research to determine who should receive your "cc's." Again, your local librarian can help you locate trade organizations and government agencies. The list on Alan Condit's letter offers several relevant suggestions.

Prudent Use of the "CC"

As we said earlier, however, copies are like trump cards. You don't want to play them all at once. Nor do you want to use them frivolously. If, for instance, your complaint involves a faulty toothbrush or popcorn popper, the state attorney general is not likely to be interested. Indeed, he or she would be offended that you would bother him or her with such a trivial problem.

This is important to keep in mind. Remember the story of the boy who cried wolf? Calls for help—and that's exactly what copies of a complaint letter sent to third parties are—should be used judiciously and only when necessary. Alan Condit first gave Mr. Fischer a chance to remedy the problem. And even when he had to write a second, stronger letter, he did not play all of his cards at once.

We recommend such handling of the "cc," and complaints in general. First, give the offending party a chance to rectify the situation. In many cases this will be the quickest and easiest solution. Go directly to the salesperson or clerk, or to the local manager, either in person or by phone. We have found that most people are willing to be helpful in solving problems with service or merchandise.

If this doesn't work, or if the clerk is part of the problem, then it's time to go to the owner or president. Again, this route is usually all it takes to get your complaint addressed satisfactorily. Sending copies of the first letter, to your local Chamber of Commerce for instance, or to an attorney, could be jumping the gun. This tactic *may* be necessary to speed things up if you're in a big hurry. If you are not, give the president or owner a chance to make good. He or she could turn out to be quite reasonable and willing to work with you to solve your complaint.

It would be embarrassing if, after the problem is taken care of, the state agency you "cc'd" started to investigate. They may be unhappy with you for not pursuing every avenue possible before seeking outside help. After all, most government organizations are understaffed and overworked these days, and they often resent having their time wasted.

On the other hand, if the top person in the offending company or business is uncooperative, it's time to send out the copies. But again, a note of caution. Even when the copies become necessary, choose your recipients wisely. Don't bother large and powerful organizations with relatively trivial problems.

For example, let's say you have a problem with a used car dealership. You write a letter to the owner and "cc" it to the state and federal attorney generals.

You'll probably be disappointed. It's very unlikely that these two busy people will have time to address your problem—and the owner of the dealership knows that. Copies sent to the district attorney's office, a trade association, or a local consumer advocate group will likely have a greater effect.

Another point to remember: involving government agencies and trade organizations in trivial problems can strip you of your credibility. The toothbrush example we used earlier comes to mind. Problems of this small magnitude can almost always be solved with the manufacturer or local dealer. Sending out copies to government agencies, especially with a first letter, may make you look silly. Later, if a big problem comes along when you really do need their help, they may remember you—but not in a positive way. You may find your letter shuffled to the bottom of the pile.

When they are used correctly, though, copies constitute a powerful part of your arsenal of weapons. Here's a case that demonstrates how a broadening base of "cc's" can finally motivate an offending party to take action on your behalf.

Auto Repair Blues

An acquaintance of ours experienced a problem with an auto repair shop. Though she was charged a great deal of money, her car didn't seem to perform any better than before she had taken it in for repair. Furthermore, she felt that because she didn't know much about automobiles, she had been misled as to the nature of the problem. She strongly suspected that parts that were supposed to have been replaced, and for which she was charged, had not been changed. When her complaints fell on deaf ears at the shop, she wrote a strong letter to the owner. The response she received was not satisfactory, so she wrote the following letter:

May 3, 1993

Gary Manhausen
Central Auto Repair
1997 23rd Ave. NW
Cincinnati, OH 42448

Mr. Manhausen:

Your response to my letter of April 23 was not at all satisfactory. I certainly do intend to go to another repair shop, but not until the work you charged me for has been completed, and not until I have been assured that the parts you charged me for were indeed installed.

Frankly, I am shocked at your cavalier attitude. I don't see how you can remain in business when you make no effort to satisfy your customers and, even more seriously, charge them in a fraudulent manner.

Please see to it that my car is properly repaired.

Impatiently,

Ellen Deys
8286 Kyleson Rd.
Cincinnati, OH 42436

cc: District Attorney
American Association of Automobile Repair
Cincinnati Chamber of Commerce

When this letter received no answer, she drafted and sent a third:

May 14, 1993

Gary Manhausen
Central Auto Repair
1997 23rd Ave. NW
Cincinnati, OH 42448

Mr. Manhausen:

You have been remarkably uncooperative. I have lost patience with you. I will settle for nothing less than a full refund of my $325.56, and an additional $134.89 for a rental car and towing charges on the car you supposedly fixed.

Any further communications from me will be through my attorney.

Ellen Deys

cc: District Attorney
Chamber of Commerce

American Association of Automobile Repair
State Licensing Board
Jacobson, Meyers, and Wilson
Channel 5 Consumer Action

Ten days after sending this letter, Ms. Deys received a check for $460.00 from Manhausen. Though her dogged insistence on being treated fairly must have been a factor, we believe it was Ms. Dey's increasing list of "cc's" that finally prompted Manhausen to act. It may well have been the last "cc" on her list that did the trick; no company wants its name lambasted over the airwaves. Something like that can kill a business, and Manhausen knew it. It was worth $460.00 to avoid the bad publicity, especially when it was clear that Ms. Deys was not going to give up.

As these examples have demonstrated, you have many weapons at your disposal for getting action on a complaint. Sometimes, however, no matter how insistent you are, the offending individual or organization will not respond satisfactorily. In Chapter 9 we'll discuss what to do when complaining to the source of your problem doesn't work.

In the meantime, we'll assume you agree that writing is the most effective way to deal with complaints. But what if you feel that your writing is poor, and you have no confidence in your ability to get your message across clearly? You're not alone!

The next chapter will put your fears to rest. Writing the perfect complaint letter is easier than you think!

4

Putting Your
Protest on Paper

A friend of ours once experienced a problem with a mail-order company. She finally got so disgusted with its poor service that she decided to write a complaint letter to the president of the company. But when she sat down to write, the words wouldn't come. She didn't know how to start. Ultimately, she gave up, more angry at her lack of writing ability than at the company!

We've heard stories like this more often than we can count. For many people, writing is a grueling chore to be avoided at all costs. Why should this be? Probably because most people still write with their high school English teacher staring over their shoulder! They remember being forced to write on stultifyingly dull subjects, handing papers in, and then getting them back with more red than black on the page. From this experience they learned that writing was (1) hard, (2) no fun, and (3) a lost cause unless you are a "natural" writer.

Hogwash! These are three of the most famous writing myths. Unfortunately, many people still believe them, even people like scientists and corporate executives. These myths stifle writing, suffocate creativity, and are a major cause of writer's block. In this chapter you will learn *why* these beliefs are myths and how you can defeat them.

THE SPEAKWRITE™ SYSTEM

As we noted in Chapter 1, many people will complain heartily to their neighbor, their spouse, or their dog. But when it comes to writing to someone who can do something about their problem, they are suddenly mute. That's because they don't know where to start. Most people are under the mistaken impression that they are supposed to produce perfect copy the first time. Since they know they can't do that, they consider themselves failures at writing. They balk at the thought of trying to express themselves in writing. Yet these same people have no trouble *talking* about their problems!

Thats why we developed the SPEAKWRITE system. SPEAKWRITE is based on the premise that, if you can speak it, you can write it. It's really that simple. Our minds organize thought patterns into logical speech every day, by:

- *PLANNING*
- *SPEAKING*
- *CLARIFYING*

There is no reason why that same ability can't be used in writing. In fact, SPEAKWRITE uses a similar system:

- *PLANNING*
- *WRITING*
- *REFINING*

We are going to tap into your brain's already existing system to show you how writing with sparkle and snap can be both easy and fun. We'll take it one step at a time.

Planning

When the mind is formulating thoughts in preparation for speech, we are hardly aware of it. We know what we want to say, and we say it. In reality, the brain is going through a very complex process of generating ideas and making connections between them. That is precisely what SPEAKWRITE does in its planning stage.

Often when people have to write something, they try to outline it first, as they were taught in school. But in fact, outlining during the planning stage is exactly the *wrong* thing to do. If outlining is what you were taught, forget it! Outlining is an analytical, left-brain activity. It takes already existing ideas and orgranizes them coherently, It is a very useful technique—*once the ideas have been generated*. But how can you determine the order of your ideas before you have them all in front of you? Trying to organize ideas before they exist is absurd!

If you are more comfortable dictating than writing, speak your ideas into a tape recorder to help you sort them. Then play back the tape and jot down any relevant ideas you've dictated. Once you sort them out, you can dictate them again onto the tape as an alternative to freewriting on your paper or personal computer.

In our experience, the more visual people are, the more they feel comfortable writing. Auditory people enjoy taping or dictating to get them started. Most important, find the method that works best for you—and enjoy the process.

The planning stage of SPEAKWRITE uses techniques designed to take advantage of the way the brain works. These techniques are the following:

- **BRAINSTORMING**
- **MINDMAPPING**
- **FREEWRITING**

Brainstorming is one of the most effective methods for getting your ideas on paper before you try to organize, reorganize, or compose the letter. It is an unstructured, free associative process and a powerful way to "loosen up" so you can be creative.

Most people compose with two voices inside their head competing for attention. One is the writer, creative and uncensored; the other is the editor, critical and judgmental. The problem is that the editor appears too early in most people's writing process. The editor's favorite phrase is "That sounds

" The critical power . . . tends to make an intellectual situation of which the creative power can profitably avail itself . . . to make the best ideas prevail. "

—Matthew Arnold
1822-1888

The Function of Criticism at the Present Time [1864]

stupid." This voice vetoes too many ideas before they ever get on paper. That's not to say that the editor isn't necessary. Editing is a vital part of the revision process, but it's nothing but trouble in the planning stage.

During this first stage, when you're deciding on what you want want to say, be lenient with yourself. It's a relaxed time. No one's looking—not your family, your boss, your friends, not even your high school teacher! Let yourself go. You'll discover that you're more creative than you ever thought.

Brainstorming.   Brainstorming is simply the process of jotting down whatever ideas come to you, in whatever order they come to you. For example, a friend of ours had to write a letter to an insurance company a short time ago, requesting a refund for a canceled policy. She had purchased insurance for a motorcycle at one rate, but was then charged a higher rate. When the problem couldn't be straightened out she canceled the policy. Yet, the insurance company sent her only a small fraction of the refund she was due, claiming some unclear "administrative policy" as their justification. She was furious, and she decided to write a complaint letter. Here's a possible brainstorm of her ideas:

---

not fair! paying thousands equivalent!

paid $306 June 30

charged 25 year old rate

Pete Hansen told no problem

$306 is total amount

mid-July, bill for $108.68

Called Hansen—selling company
turned over to Jean Sanders—bill a mistake
would look into and call

August—another bill for $283.68 (includes 108.68 + 175.00!!)

keep getting bills!

not sure about this motorcycle business

breathing smog

Jean Sanders—must pay 24 year old rate!

Canceled

refund check for $18.40

administrative early cancel policy?

As you can see, this is essentially a random list of ideas pertaining to the complaint. You wouldn't necessarily use all of them, but it's a good idea to write everything down. Plus, you'll find that one idea will trigger another. The more ideas you come up with, the greater the range and depth of your thoughts. Then, when it comes time to write, you have more to choose from.

Mindmapping. Another powerful technique is mindmapping. Like brainstorming, mindmapping mimics the freeflowing way your brain sorts information. You start with a central thought, placed in the middle of a page, then branch your ideas off this core idea. Mindmapping is sometimes referred to as clustering, because the mind clusters related ideas together instead of sorting them in a linear form. That's why in school most of us wrote our papers first and outlined them afterwards. Again, how could you know your order of ideas before you saw them in front of you?

Here are some guidelines to mindmapping:

- *Draw a square or circle in the middle of the page.*
- *Inside, jot down the subject of your writing.*
- *Draw branches from the circle for different but related ideas.*
- *Use the journalist's technique of asking yourself who, what, when, where, why, and how for generating ideas.*
- *Branch off from the main ideas into smaller, related topics.*

A mindmap of the insurance problem might look like this:

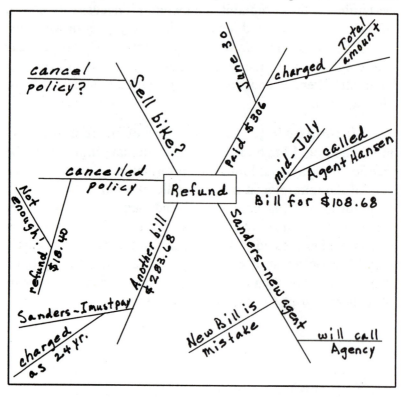

After you've finished your mindmap, you'll want to establish the priorities of your ideas, numbering them in the order you want them presented in your letter. The rule here is to put the main idea first, and let the rest follow. Requests and conclusions should come before justifications and discussions. We'll talk more about letter organization in Chapter 5.

Freewriting your complaint.   Once your ideas and facts are all in front of you, and the priorities established, it's easier to organize your thoughts for writing the first draft. For that we turn to freewriting.

Freewriting is probably the most powerful tool the writer has at his or her disposal. Freewriting means exactly what it sounds like: writing without stopping, without thinking about it, and above all, without editing.

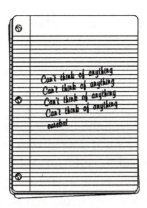

Here's what you do: Pick up a pen or start up your word processor and begin writing. Don't stop to think about what you want to say; just write. If you can't think of what to write, write that! Write the phrase "can't think of anything" over and over until something else comes out!

Thinking is hard work, and since writing involves thinking, our minds put up roadblocks to keep us from moving. Writing the same word or phrase over and over short-circuits this system. Sooner or later your subconscious gets bored and gives in. Suddenly, you find the ideas flowing as fast as you can write them down. If you do this technique correctly, it is a guaranteed cure for writer's block.

As you freewrite, don't make any changes, don't go back and add anything between the lines, and *don't* start over. Ignore punctuation and spelling mistakes. Just let your thoughts flow freely. You'll have plenty of time later to go back and revise. Your mind may wander off the subject occasionally (as our minds have a tendency to do!) but don't worry about it. Just keep writing. The important thing is to get everything down. In a nutshell:

- *Write without stopping.*
- *Create without editing.*
- *Allow no criticizing.*
- *Let it sit!*

Here is a freewrite of the insurance example we've been using:

i was told that, even tho i was 24, since i was about to turn 25,and since the polisy wouldn't take effect until after i had turned 25, that i would be charged the 25 year old rate. i paid 306 to pete Hansen. (he's the one who explained all this). but then i got aditional bill for 108. what gives, i thought. so i called hansen, but he had turned over the agancy to jean sanders. She said it was obviously a mistake (of course) and would look into it and call me back. THEN in august i get another bill for 283, which is the 108 plus 175. You guys keep sending me bills!! getting pretty fed up with the whole business at this point. besides, riding around here on the freeways is not much fun—breathing all those fumes. not as much fun as i thought it would be. jean sanders said i would have to pay rate of 24 year old—even tho i was now 25! baloney! I canceled. a few weeks later i get my refund: 18 dollars! For six weeks i paid 288!! called JS—she said it was company policy—early withdrawal penalties or some such nonsense. what is this-a bank? this is not fair. i should get refund of at least 270.

As you can see, this is essentially a stream-of-consciousness piece of writing. That is the essence of freewriting. The thoughts and ideas flow out in whatever order your mind gives them to you. From there you're ready to make some choices about what to include in your letter, and what to leave out. Then it's time to organize the ideas and start writing.

Writing

This is the stage that stops most people dead in their tracks. Getting the ideas down is one thing, they think; writing them so they sound intelligent is quite another.

Not so! Actually, the transition is an easy one to make. The first thing to do is to go back to your freewrite sample and locate the *most important idea.* What is the purpose of the letter? Is it to let off steam, or is it to get some action? In this case, the letter writer wants a reasonable refund. Circle that idea, now at the bottom of the page. That's where we'll start.

Before we actually sit down to write, though, it's important to keep some fundamental rules in mind:

SPEAKWRITE™ Rules Of Writing

- *Decrease sentence length.*
- *Omit needless words.*
- *Avoid stuffy language.*
- *Use strong verbs.*

We call these the SPEAKWRITE Rules of Writing. They have helped thousands of our students make the change from struggling over a letter to nearly effortless writing. If you stick to these rules, they can help your writing become clear and forceful. Let's look at each one briefly.

Decrease sentence length. If you're like us, you were taught in school that "longer is better." We were encouraged to fluff and puff up our sentences with verbiage and expand our essays—whether we actually said anything or not! Well, now is the time to toss out that rule. When you are writing for effect, *shorter is* better. Long, convoluted sentences are difficult to read and difficult to comprehend. The last thing you want to do is make your reader struggle through your complaint letter. Be concise. Keep your sentences to 20 words or less whenever possible. A good average to aim for is 14 to 17 words per sentence. You should also vary your sentence length for added effect. The shorter the sentence, often the more powerful the thought.

A quick, easy way to test your sentence length is to count the number of lines per sentence. If a sentence runs over two printed lines in a document, it's probably too long. Also, read your sentences aloud. If you have to take more than one breath, your sentence is too long.

One good way to cut back on length is to look for the word "and." Many writers have what we call "and-itis." See if this type of construction sounds familiar:

> As I mentioned, and I know you understand, I am willing to be flexible in this matter, and to give you the benefit of the doubt and all my cooperation in coming to a solution which is equitable and fair to all parties concerned, and to see to it that this awkward and unpleasant situation does not arise again, and I thank you for your patience.

Quite a mouthful! Yet many people write this way, never knowing where to stop. Clearly, this sentence could be broken up several ways, just by getting rid of a few "and"s. Here's one possible revision:

> I am willing to be flexible in this matter. I'll
> give you my full cooperation in coming to a
> solution that is fair to all concerned, and I'll
> see to it that this problem does not arise
> again. Thanks for your patience.

These three sentences are much more concise and easy to read. In addition, you'll notice that we use fewer words to say the same thing, and say it better. More on reducing words in a moment.

For now, try not to cover too many thoughts in one sentence by stringing them together with the word "and." One of the most neglected punctuation marks is the period. Use it! After one complete idea, stop and put a period. Then go on to the next thought. If you need to, use transition words like *nevertheless, also,* and *however* to bridge thoughts. Transitions can be very useful, as long as they're not overused.

Again, it is a good idea to vary your sentence length and structure. Sentences that are all roughly the same length and style tend to bore the reader, much as a monotone speaker will put his or her audience to sleep.

Another way to break up sentences is to use lists. Listing, or "bulleting," has the added advantage of putting emphasis on your points. Take this example:

> I lost over $500 in sales because your
> employees put the wrong part in my car,
> delayed obtaining the correct part from the
> manufacturer, and, to make matters worse,
> broke another part while fixing the first.

This sentence would be stronger and clearer if the information were listed. To set up a list, bullet your individual points by putting a symbol, such as -, *, or o before each one. We prefer the small "o," as it is a clear and easily recognized mark.

Unless your list is a step-by-step procedure, avoid numbering your items. Numbering gives the first items a priority that may not be appropriate. Also, we recommend starting each item in a list with a verb if possible. That gives the list more power:

> *I lost over $500 in sales because your employees:*
> o *Installed the wrong part in my car*
> o *Delayed obtaining the right part*
> o *Broke another part while fixing the first.*

The ideas in the sentence are now more clearly presented and easier to read.

Omit needless words. In school, we were all given a writing assignment and told that it had to be a certain length. Because we couldn't always come up with enough to say on the subject, we learned to "fluff up" our writing with extra words—words and phrases like "in all actuality," "in the amount of," "at this point in time," "interestingly," and "amazingly enough." These words are fillers. They serve no purpose but to lengthen a piece of writing. Get rid of them! They don't belong in a complaint letter. Look at this example:

> After speaking with all the parties involved, and discussing the issue at length for days, we decided that, at this point in time, it was time that we should take a stand. In actual fact, this decision should have been made expeditiously by us several weeks ago, but we were hastily rushing around filling back orders and, to put it mildly, did not have the time to devote to carefully organizing a complaint, and we apologize for the delay. Therefore, we would like a refund, per your quotation, in the amount of $3,000.

Truly awful! Yet we see writing like this all the time. The paragraph is full of "fluff" words, unnecessary modifiers, "anditis," and redundancies. Now compare the following revision for clarity:

> We discussed the issue at length and decided we would like a refund of $3,000. We apologize for the delay in responding to you, but we have been quite busy.

We were able to go from 93 words to 30, an elimination of 63 words! At the same time, we have vastly improved the clarity of the ideas. Keep this in mind when you are doing your own writing. Avoid wind-up phrases like "after speaking with all the parties involved," "per your request of," "in response to your letter," or "while in anticipation of." Many writers seem to have this need to ease themselves into sentences with phrases that add no meaning to the sentence. You don't need them. They just bog the reader down. Get to the point of the sentence without a lengthy "wind-up" as justification.

Also, watch out for adverbs. (Most adverbs end in *ly*, so they're easy to pick out.) Strong verbs don't need help from words like "quickly," "smoothly," or "really." Certainly, adverbs are useful parts of speech, and used judiciously they can add style to your writing. But don't overdo it!

Another grammatical construction to avoid is the prepositional phrase. This is a phrase beginning with "of," "in," "about," or any other preposition: "of the opinion," "in the future," "about the offer." Prepositional phrases can really clog up a piece of writing. For example, "the son of the brother of the father of the writer of this sentence" is just a convoluted way of saying "my cousin." Even "a cousin of mine" is unnecessarily bulky. "My cousin" says it all with half the words.

Prepositional phrases can abound in writing. They are particularly popular with attorneys and bureaucrats—people who write "party of the first part" and similar expressions. We all have had to struggle through documents and forms full of such phrases. No one enjoys it. It's difficult and time-consuming. Yet many people believe that writing this way makes them sound official. In our opinion, it just sounds silly. If you don't want to sound like you write income-tax forms or legal briefs for a living, use prepositional phrases sparingly.

Finally, try to avoid stating the obvious—that is, phrases like "he is the man who works for your company." Obviously, "he" is a man. What else would "he" be? Try "he works for your company." It's much clearer and to the point.

Basically, our rule is this: Keep the essential words and throw out the rest.

Avoid stuffy language.   This rule is the cornerstone of the SPEAKWRITE system. The idea that writing must be fancy to be effective is outdated. In fact, ornate, fancy, overblown writing crammed to the margins with $10-dollar words usually has the opposite effect: it makes the writer sound pompous and pretentious. So stay away from phrases like "optimal transitional projection" or "systematized organizational flexibility." They don't mean anything to anyone! Rely on commonly understood words to make your point.

INSTEAD OF:	WRITE:
assistance	help
remuneration	pay
commence	start
utilize	use
enclosed please find	here's

Don't say "It is necessary that your response be received by me by June 10" when you can write "I must have your answer by June 10." Write to express, not to impress. Use language that does not call attention to itself. Ask yourself, "How would I say this?" Then write it that way. Avoid turning nouns into verbs by adding "-ize" to the end. Examples are operationalize, prioritize, maximize, and systematize. The best they can do is obscure your meaning. Compare the next two letters.

Dear Mr. Smith:

Please find enclosed a copy of your invoice number 2283, as of 23 July 1993. Be advised that we will be unable to effect remuneration of this invoice pending your completion of the work delineated in our contractual agreement. In particular, installation of the workspace delimiters is critical if we are to operationalize our accounts/receivable department. Pending outcome of this contract and the work described therein, your continued association with this firm remains under advisement.

Sincerely,

Mr. Jones

What a mess! If you struggled through this letter, imagine how a busy corporate executive might react to a complaint letter written in the same manner! Keep it simple! Here's what Mr. Jones was trying to say:

Dear Mr. Smith:

Here's a copy of your invoice (#2283) dated July 23, 1993. I'm afraid we must withhold payment on this invoice until you complete the work listed in our contract. We would like you to install the room dividers immediately, so that our accounting department can begin work.

If you do not complete this job soon, we may not call on you for our future needs.

Sincerely,

Mr. Jones

Here's another example of how stuffy language can obscure meaning:

It is a certainty that one may, given the inclination, convey an equine quadruped into the general vicinity of an aqueous reservoir; however, inducing said artiodactyl to imbibe same aforesaid aqueous solution, given the beast's occasional disinclination, is quite another matter altogether.

Were you able to make out this proverb?

"You can lead a horse to water, but you can't make him drink."

Write the way you speak!

Use strong verbs. Verbs create power in your writing. The central word in your sentence is the verb. It's the action word, the one that moves the sentence along. The last thing you want to do in a letter demanding action is to use weak verbs. Instead of "Your new assistant is negligent in her work" write "Your new assistant neglects her work." Try to limit your use of the verb *to be,* in all its forms: *am, is, are, was, were, will be, can,* or *should be.* Also, don't overuse infinitives such as *to do, to make, to seem, to appear, to be,* and *to get.* They are all weak, powerless verbs.

Of course, you can't avoid these weak verbs all the time, nor would you want to. If you simply become aware of the verbs you're using and try to choose strong ones whenever possible, your writing will have more power.

Also, we recommend that you avoid using the passive voice. Passive and active voice can be understood in this way: think of the people you know. Passive people let things happen to them; active people make things happen. It's the same with sentences. For example, instead of using this sentence in the passive voice:

The authorization for refund was given to me by your clerk.

write:

> **Your clerk authorized the refund.**

The second sentence is much more direct and economical. It also eliminates the "being" verb.

When you're writing, ask yourself, "Who's doing what to whom?"

> **My television was inspected by the store supervisor.**

Who's supposed to be the actor in this sentence? The supervisor, of course. So change the word order to reflect this:

> **The store supervisor inspected my television.**

This switch does three important things. First, it changes the sentence from passive to active. Second, it eliminates the weak "being" verb and substitutes an active, strong verb, "inspected." And third, it tightens and shortens the sentence.

Watch your own writing for passivity and eliminate it whenever possible.

Putting it all together. Now, with these simple rules in mind, let's go back to that budding complaint letter about motorcycle insurance. Here's a first draft:

Dear Mr. Jensen:

On June 30, I bought a motorcycle policy from
one of your agents, Pete Hansen. At the time I
bought it, I was three days away from my 25th
birthday. Mr. Hansen told me that, since I was
about to turn 25, and since the policy would
take a few days to be processed, and wouldn't
go into effect until after I was 25, I would
pay the same rate as a 25 year old. So I paid
him $306 for a year's coverage. Then, in the
middle of July I received a bill from Pacific
Insurance for another $108.68. I didn't under-
stand what that was all about, so I called Pete
Hansen back. He had since sold the agency to a
woman named Jean Sanders. She told me that it
must be a mistake and she would look into it.

Then in early August I received yet another
bill from Pacific Insurance, this one for
$283.68, which was the original $108.68 plus an
additional $175. I called Jean Sanders again
and she told me that it was no mistake, and
that I would have to pay the bill if I wanted
to retain the policy. I had to pay the same
rate as a 24-year-old, even though I am now 25.
This didn't seem fair to me, so I told Jean
Sanders that I wanted to cancel the policy. She
said the balance of my policy would be refunded.

On September 19, I received a refund check for
$18.40! When I called Jean Sanders about this,
she said that it was company policy, that there
were penalties for early cancellation. This
seems like a pretty severe penalty to me! Why
should I pay if the conditions of my policy
have been misrepresented? I don't think it is
fair at all, and I think I should get a bigger
refund. I will be waiting to hear from you.

Sincerely,

Elizabeth Gallway

This is not a bad letter, but it is lengthy and wordy. Several improvements could and should be made. This brings us to the final step in the SPEAKWRITE process.

Refining

Many people take our writing classes thinking they will learn to turn out perfect copy in a first draft. Though it is possible, after years and years of practice, to turn out a perfect letter the first time you sit down to write, this is the exception rather than the rule. All experienced writers know that good writing depends on *rewriting* more than on any other factor.

Once you have written the first draft of your letter, there are many things you can do to ensure that it says what you really want it to. First, ask yourself these questions:

- *Have I written for the audience I want to address?*
- *Have I used an appropriate tone?*
- *Is my language appropriate? Is it natural and comfortable? How would I say this if I were speaking?*
- *Are my verbs strong and active?*
- *Have I made my point? Have I asked for what I want?*
- *Have I followed the SPEAKWRITE Rules of Writing?*
- *Does the letter look presentable?*

Let's take a look at Ms. Gallway's letter. The tone here is generally appropriate, though it is more emotional than professional. A few minor alterations in the wording can fix that. For the most part, the language is appropriate.

Most of the verbs are strong and active. However, in three important places she uses "seem" or "should." Stronger verbs would work better.

What about her point? We think it could be made more emphatically. In the first place, it is located at the bottom of the letter, just as it was in her freewriting sample. It's much more effective to make your point early and justify it later (see Chapter 5). Further, Ms. Gallway is not exactly clear on what she wants. Her demand is only for a vague "bigger" refund. She needs to be more specific.

Does the letter look right? How a letter looks is very important. A verbose letter is less likely to be read. The paragraphs in this letter are too long. They look heavy and formidable. They should be broken up to give the letter more white space. Also, there are a few grammatical and spelling errors that need to be corrected.

Regarding SPEAKWRITE rules: most of Ms. Gallway's sentences are shorter than 20 words; in fact, only two are longer than that. The average is about 15 words. Also, she has varied the length of her sentences nicely.

There are, however, a few places where words could be omitted. There is also some repetition. The word "pay" is used several times, for instance. In addition, the wording is not as clear as it could be and she rambles at times. The language sounds natural, though, and isn't stuffy. As we said earlier, the verbs are generally strong.

The all-important rewrite.   Once you've gone over your letter and identified the areas that need improvement, it's time to rewrite. Many people, however, are reluctant to make major changes in their writing. They seem to feel that once they've written something down, it's etched in concrete.

That is both false and ridiculous. Nothing is sacred. You must be willing to change anything and everything if it will make your letter better and more effective. Here is Ms. Gallway's final draft:

October 1, 1993

Elizabeth Gallway
3445 Wilbur Street
San Diego, CA 92119

Richard Jensen, President
Pacific Insurance
2214 North Allan Ave.
Downey, CA 92664

Dear Mr. Jensen:

A situation has come up that deserves your attention. I recently paid $306 for a Pacific policy on a motorcycle. I was forced to cancel the policy after six weeks, yet I received only $18.40 in refund. Mr. Jensen, this is very unfair. I believe Pacific owes me another $252.29. Here's why:

I bought my policy from one of your agents, Pete Hansen, on June 30, 1993, three days before my 25th birthday. Mr. Hansen assured me that, because it would take a few days for the policy to be processed, I would pay the rate charged to policy holders over 25 years old. I paid him $306 for a full year's coverage. He told me this was the total amount I would have to pay.

In mid-July I received a bill from Pacific for an additional $108.68. When I informed the new owner of the agency, Jean Sanders, she told me that it was obviously a mistake and that she would take care of it.

In early August I received a second bill, one for $283.68. This bill included the July $108.68 plus another $175. I phoned the agent again, and she told me that I would have to pay the amount charged to a 24-year-old, *even though I was then 25.*

It was clear to me at that point that I had been deceived, and that the conditions of my policy had been misrepresented. I felt I had no choice but to cancel the policy. Jean Sanders told me that my balance would be refunded. Then, on September 22, I received a refund check for $18.40.

I'm sure you will agree, Mr. Jensen, that this is very unfair. In effect, your company is charging me the equivalent of $2500 per year for the six weeks I was insured! So I am returning the check uncashed. I believe I am entitled to a total refund of $270.69.

I trust you will give your prompt attention to this matter and bring it to a just and fair conclusion. I look forward to hearing from you soon.

Sincerely,

Elizabeth Gallway

This version reads easier and looks better. Ms. Gallway's demands are much more firm and specific, and the sequence of events is clearer. More important, she has first stated what she wanted and then justified it. Mr. Jensen didn't have to weed through the whole letter to find out what it was about.

Ms. Gallway did several other things that increased the chances of Jensen acting in her favor. For one, she extrapolated her situation to show the absurdity of it. Sometimes people get caught up in their regulations and "policy" and lose sight of the realities. Ms. Gallway brought that home by simply calculating what she had *really* been charged, above and beyond the $306.

Second, she sent the check back uncashed. This action forced the insurance company to do something. They *had* to deal with her, since her policy could not be considered closed.

Proofreading—the final touch.   Before your letter is put in the mail, there is one more thing to do: proofread. This is a critical step. You don't want your letters going out with spelling and grammatical errors. Here are a few proofreading tips that will help ensure perfect copy each time:

- *Let it sit:* Never proofread just after writing. You're too familiar with your words, and need time to pass so you can look at the letter objectively.

- *Read it aloud:* This will give you a new perspective. You'll hear how your words sound, and you'll pick up errors you might otherwise have missed.

- *Give it to someone else to read:* Put aside your shyness, because this step guarantees improvement. Give it to someone you trust. They'll be able to look at it much more objectively, and they can tell you what works and what doesn't.

- *Read it backwards, bottom to top:* This secretarial technique helps you spot spelling and mechanical errors. In effect, you're reading word for word, not for context or meaning.

- *Use reference materials, like dictionaries, writing references, and punctuation handbooks:* Even the best writers rely on outside materials to double-check themselves occasionally. We've included a list of reference books in the bibliography.

- *Use spelling checkers:* Most software programs have this feature. We strongly suggest that you use it. However, remember that it can't correct misspelled names, misused homonyms (waist/waste), or transposed letters (used/sued).

Once you've completed these steps and any further rewriting that results, your letter is ready to mail. Two weeks after mailing hers, Elizabeth Gallway received a check from Pacific Insurance for $260.69—which was $10.00 less than what she anticipated. She wasn't aware that a $10.00 policy fee built into the premium was not refundable.

But how did she know what to ask for? We'll cover that in Chapter 5.

CHAPTER

5

How to Ask
for What
You Want

A complaint letter that merely vents frustration has no direction and little purpose. Sure, writing such a letter may make you feel good—but how much better would you feel if you received a full refund or a free travel voucher? A letter that demands and receives restitution is a lot more useful than one that merely gripes. It's important, then, when writing a complaint letter, to know what you want and how to ask for it.

KNOW WHAT YOU WANT

Take another look at Elizabeth Gallway's letter in Chapter 4. She knew before she started writing that she wanted—and deserved—a refund much greater than the one she was sent. But how much? She is not an insurance agent and doesn't know how Pacific Insurance assesses their charges.

The answer was very straightforward: Since a year's coverage cost her $306, she divided that by the number of weeks in a year (52) to give her the cost of the insurance per week. She then subtracted six week's worth of insurance from $306 and asked for the remainder. That seemed perfectly reasonable. She just didn't know about the $10.00 nonrefundable policy fee.

And this is the key to any request: It must be within reason. If you ask for the whole store, you obviously won't be taken seriously. But if you paid for an item that fails to work properly, it is certainly reasonable to ask for a refund or replacement. And if you paid for a service that you didn't receive, or that was substandard, your money should be refunded. After all, you did not get what you paid for.

Here's an example:

February 13, 1994

Mr. and Mrs. John Talley
112 Ocean Drive
Tampa, FL 33024

Chester Wankle
COUPONS '94
P.O. Box 456
Chicago, IL 66012

Dear Mr. Wankle:

We recently purchased the COUPON '94 book for use this year, as did our friends the Wilsons. This morning we made plans to use the book and meet for Sunday brunch at the Tampa Gold Room. We got there, were seated, and then learned from the waitress that the coupons were not valid and would not be honored.

It was rather embarrassing for us. Nevertheless, we stayed and ordered brunch—paying the price for all four in our party.

That tab was $33.81 (without tax). We are sending you the check stub, both our coupons, and the business card from the restaurant for your identification. We trust that you will "make good" the promise of your book—to provide a complimentary meal with each one purchased. We will look for a check from you in the amount of $16.90—half the $33.81.

Thank you for your attention to this matter.

Sincerely,

Mrs. John Talley

Like Ms. Gallway's request, Mrs. Talley's is also straightforward and perfectly reasonable. She paid for a book of coupons, one of them was worthless, and she asked that the coupon company's obligation be honored. For more examples of letters that make reasonable and valid demands, see Chapter 1.

What do you do if your complaint is not so clear-cut? What if, for instance, you are mistreated by an airline? They deliver you to your destination, but you must suffer through a horrible flight because of mismanagement or employee negligence. What should you ask for in this case?

Here's a letter from a writer who clearly didn't know the answer to that question:

June 30, 1993

Midcountry Airlines
339 Arapahoe St.
Omaha, NB 43557

Dear Sirs:

Once again I tried flying your airline. Once again, Midcountry did not let me down. You lost my luggage, and you changed planes on me. My seat—assigned a month earlier—was eliminated, and I had to move from the business class to a center seat in the smoking section. I did have a choice, of course. I could have waited for the next flight and missed a business meeting. Missing that meeting would have cost my company about $3,000,000.00. Has anyone ever sued an airline company for money lost because of a missed meeting due to your lack of concern for your customers?

In our company we do excessive business travel, and the word is that Midcountry is not a company to be trusted. We avoid using Midcountry as much as possible. I think a reevaluation of your service and attention given to your customers is in order.

Sincerely,

Robert Helms
Vice President
Singelton Data Products

This ineffective letter begs for a flaccid response, and that's exactly what it received. Midcountry apologized for Mr. Helms' inconvenience and weakly suggested that he fly the airline again. Hardly satisfying.

Mr. Helms made several errors in this letter. For one thing, he did not write to the top. Instead, he sent the letter to a nameless mid-level paper-pusher who had no power or authority to address Mr. Helms' complaint.

Second, all he did was complain—and not very effectively at that. His rhetorical question about suing airlines is too vague and unspecific to be taken seriously. Mr. Helms missed a golden opportunity to make a point *and* demand specific reparation.

What amends are appropriate in this case? Mr. Helms paid for a service that was only partly rendered. He was delivered to his destination, as promised, but at great personal discomfort and inconvenience. If an airline—or any company—promises courteous, comfortable service and then does not provide it, they have not fulfilled their end of the contract. In this case, half the airfare in refund seems reasonable to us, and that's what we would ask for. Here's how we would do it:

June 30, 1993

William Pender
President
Midcountry Airlines
339 Arapahoe St.
Omaha, NB 43557

Dear Mr. Pender:

My last flight on your airline was unsatisfactory. You delivered me to my destination, but
under conditions quite different from those
specified in our contract (the ticket). Therefore, I would like you to refund at least half
the purchase price of my ticket ($458.00).

This is what happened: First, after reserving
and paying for a business-class ticket a month
in advance, I found that you had changed planes,
and my reserved seat no longer existed. I was
shuffled to the smoking section in the back of
the plane. I didn't have much choice. Had I
waited for the next flight, I would have missed
an important business meeting—at a potential
loss to my company of $3,000,000.00.

Second, you lost my luggage—and this is not the
first time that has happened. Frankly, I am
becoming discouraged with the service you provide. Executives of my company travel extensively, and we have used Midcountry frequently
in the past. However, unless your service improves, we will be forced to avoid your airline
in the future.

For now, I look forward to an apology and a
check for $229.00.

Sincerely,

Robert Helms
Vice President
Singelton Data Products

This letter makes the same point, but in a more business-like, less petulant manner. Further, it makes a specific demand. We would also be certain to include copies of the ticket and the boarding passes. Chances are very good that Mr. Helms would have received his check for $229, along with a personal apology from the president. Why settle for less?

So the point is, know what you want before you start writing. Be specific. Decide what dollar amount you want refunded or what specific action you want taken; then ask for it. Again, it is important to be reasonable and fair. In the preceding case, asking for a full refund is not called for, since Mr. Helms *was* delivered to his destination. By asking for half the ticket price, he's more likely to receive it. If he were completely unreasonable and asked for $1,000 or some other absurd figure in an effort to punish the airline, he'd be unlikely to receive anything.

Be reasonable and fair, and you'll probably get what you want.

HOW TO ASK FOR IT

Many people feel they must launch into a long, involved narrative regarding their situation before they get to the point. That is exactly the wrong approach. Ask for what you want early in the letter and follow up later with your reasons. Think of the structure of your letter as an inverted pyramid.

FIGURE 2

ORGANIZATION

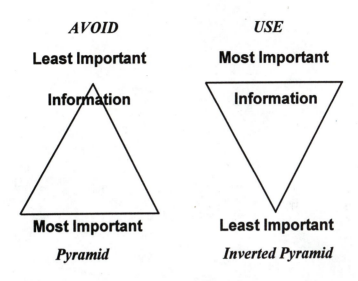

The foundation of the inverted pyramid is the principle of *inductive reasoning.* Simply stated, your request or conclusion comes first, your justifications and reasons later. The opposite is *deductive reasoning,* which leaves the most important information for last, building toward some sort of climax. While this second technique might work fine in a novel or movie, it doesn't work well in a complaint letter. Busy corporate presidents don't have time to wade through your letter looking for the bottom line.

As often as you can, organize your complaint letters as journalists do, with the most important information up front.

That's the critical difference between writing to inform (inverted pyramid) and writing to entertain (pyramid). After you've completed your draft, find the most important point, circle it, and put it as close to the beginning of your letter as you can.

Whenever possible, put:

- **Requests** *before* **justifications**
- **Conclusions** *before* **discussions**
- **Summaries** *before* **details**
- **Generalities** *before* **specifics.**

Remember, you're not writing a mystery story! The people you write to are busy. Get to the point quickly. Then follow with whatever explanations are necessary.
Take a look at the following letter:

April 12, 1994

Ms. Roseann Dewar
President, Dewar Motors
1586 University
Sacramento, CA 95883

Dear Ms. Dewar:

On Monday, February 14, 1994 I purchased my new car from your dealership. At that time I agreed to purchase a car with a factory installed cassette deck. The car I took possession of (serial #1288634) did not have a cassette deck. Therefore, the dealership agreed to replace the stereo with a stereo/cassette deck. Please see the enclosed copy of the Equipment, Condition, and Warranty Release signed by Mr. Simpson and myself. At that time I was very pleased with both my purchase and the way I had been treated at your dealership.

Unfortunately, a number of things have happened since then that have altered this pleasure. I still enjoy my car and believe it is a fine product. This is my second car from your company. However, unless I obtain *both* a cassette deck and more importantly, an explanation for the way I have been treated as a customer, I have no recourse but to have my car serviced at another dealership, to purchase any other cars from another dealership, to announce and publicize my acute displeasure with the way I have been treated by Dewar Motors, and to begin legal proceedings.

I have recorded the specific details of the problems I have encountered dealing with your employees, and have enclosed a copy of this record for your information. I also would like to point out that I received only polite and courteous help from the saleswoman, Ms. Robinson and from the service advisor Ms. Olsen. Unfortunately, it was apparent that neither of these people had the authority to make any final decisions. In contrast, the other people I dealt with, including Mr. Goodwin and Mr. Williams, whom I perceived had the authority to help me, were evasive and rude. Furthermore, in my last conversation with Mr. Williams on April 6, 1994 he was vindictive, vulgar and verbally abusive with me.

I hope that this conflict can be resolved as quickly as possible in a more productive and adult manner. I am awaiting your reply.

Sincerely,

Helen Moresby
Enclosures

Whew! If you were able to struggle through this treatise, you probably noticed several mistakes. Besides the grammatical and punctuation errors, Ms. Moresby's letter is wordy and repetitive. Worse, the main point is buried in the second paragraph, tacked on to the front of a lengthy and ineffective threat. If you were Ms. Dewar, how would you react? Would you even bother reading it?

There's a better way. Look at this possible rewrite:

Dear Ms. Dewar:

Until now, I have been happy with the service I have received from your dealership. I am no longer. I have waited nearly two months for a cassette deck to be installed, and I feel I have waited long enough. I'm asking you to see to it that the cassette deck is installed by Friday of next week. Further, I demand a written apology from your sales manager, Mr. Williams.

I purchased my new car from your dealership on February 14 of this year, and I am quite pleased with it. I am pleased also with the courteous attention given me by Ms. Olsen and Ms. Robinson. However, I am very displeased with the treatment I've received from Mr. Goodwin and, in particular, Mr. Williams. He has consistently refused to give me the service I paid for. And the last time I spoke with him, Mr. Williams was vulgar and verbally abusive toward me.

Ms. Dewar, this is no way to treat a steady customer such as myself. In the past two months I've endured numerous phone calls, several wasted trips to your dealership, and vindictive insults. I'm confident that, had you been aware of my situation earlier, none of this would have happened.

Now that you do know, I am certain that my cassette deck will be installed promptly and that my unpleasant experience with your employees will not be repeated.

I look forward to hearing from you by May 1.

Sincerely,

Ellen Moresby
Enclosures

Did you notice how this letter gets to the point quickly without beating around the bush? It makes no idle threats, but merely states in a clear, businesslike manner what is required to settle the problem. Further, it uses simpler language and a more positive tone. After all, the events described were not Ms. Dewar's fault. It is to Ms. Moresby's advantage to get Ms. Dewar on her side, not threaten her.

Attachments, Reference Lines, and Significant Data

One thing Ms. Moresby did do right was to include with her letter copies of all pertinent information. Attachments that document your problem and support your case lend power to your letter. This is true for any complaint letter. Copies of sales receipts, signed agreements, contracts, previous correspondence—anything relevant to your problem—should be included. These enclosures add a great deal of credibility to your complaint.

In the body of the letter itself, be sure to include all critical information—dates, times, names, reference numbers. But don't overdo it. Compare Ms. Moresby's letter with our rewrite. In the first, there is a great deal of unnecessary information, which bogs the letter down. For instance, the serial number of the car is really not relevant—especially if a copy of the sales agreement is attached. Also, it wasn't necessary to go into the details of the transaction since the equipment and warranty release explained it and was also included. If you can, let your attachments provide the details and significant data. Keep the letter itself brief and concise.

Reference lines can sometimes be used to cut down on the amount of background information you need to include in the body of your letter. These lines appear between the address and the salutation, and usually include information like account numbers, transaction numbers, and reference to previous correspondence. Here's an example:

June 30, 1993

Mr. Paul Jones
President
First State Bank
8849 Central Ave.
Philadelphia, PA 10665

RE: Account #39964-67

Dear Mr. Jones:

Though I have been generally pleased with the service I receive at your bank, I am having a problem clearing up an error in my account. I'd like you to give your attention to it.

I wrote a check on May 28 (check #387) and canceled payment on it the next day.

Nonetheless, my account was debited the amount of the check. Ms. Taylor, the manager at your Fourth Avenue branch, has refused to credit my account for the amount of the check, $246.98.

I canceled payment in plenty of time for the check to be refused. Therefore, I don't think I should be held financially accountable for errors on the part of your employees. I'm sure you'll agree. Please see to it that this problem is cleared up.

Thank you.

Sincerely,

Bob Morrison

Placed conspicuously in the reference line this way, Mr. Morrison's account number was easily accessible to the bank manager. He didn't have to search through the letter to find it.

Powerful Transitions

When you are explaining your problem, it's important that your explanation is clear and that your writing flows smoothly and logically from one thought to the next. One way to do this is to use transition words, such as *furthermore, nevertheless, finally,* and *therefore.*

Appropriate use of these words can increase the power and effectiveness of your letter. They usually work best at the beginning of sentences and paragraphs, but don't overdo it. One transition per paragraph is enough. Overuse can make your letter sound stuffy and pretentious. Use transitions sparingly.

Effective Openings and Closings

All good writers know that the most important parts of a sentence are the beginning and the end. Research has shown that readers tend to remember those parts after they've forgotten the rest. Similarly, the most important sentences in a paragraph are the first and the last. Those are the ones readers remember.

The same thing can be said about a letter. The most important parts, and the parts that will stick in a reader's mind, are the opening and the closing. Be aware of this when you are writing and especially when you are polishing your final draft.

Whenever possible, your opening should be positive and upbeat, and it should draw your reader into your letter. After reading the first line or two, your reader should want to read on. And he or she will, if you have done your job correctly.

The key to an effective opening is to arouse your reader's interest. Compare Ms. Moresby's letter with our rewrite. Ms. Moresby's first sentence merely states that she bought a car recently from the dealership. In fact, that is essentially all she says in the whole first paragraph. It's not very interesting, and, as readers, we are not compelled to continue.

Now look at the rewrite. Our first sentence is as positive as is possible under the circumstances. The qualifier "until now" gets the reader's attention, and the point is clarified in the next sentence. The president of a company receiving this letter would be compelled to read further. After all, a customer is expressing her dissatisfaction—and that's not good!

Closings are just as important as openings, if not more so. In your closing you make your final case for action, which can be done many different ways. Often, as in our rewrite of Ms. Moresby's letter, the closing is a direct appeal to the president of the company to take action. It is also an expression of confidence that this will happen, and that you will receive what you want.

For your closing, avoid negative constructions that invite the reader to disagree with you, such as "Don't you think...?" or "Wouldn't you say...?" Instead, use "I'm sure you'll agree..." or "I'm confident you will....,Your confidence that the problem will be solved invites your reader to feel the same way.

The following letter is an example of a first draft with a weak opening and closing.

May 11, 1993

Nancy Powell
9755 Afton St.
San Diego, CA 92117

Pete Hansen
Customer Service Manager
Triple C Camera
69 West 13th St.
New York, NY 10026

Dear Mr. Hansen:

I ordered three Nelson E-2 focusing screens on April 23, 1993 and received them on May 10, 1993. When I opened the box of one of the focusing screens, I noticed the screen was not placed in the plastic container correctly. It was loosely held off to the right side of the container instead of sitting snugly in the bed made to hold it. Upon further inspection, I noticed the focusing screen was scratched on the bottom left. Therefore, I am returning the scratched focusing screen as I found it, and would like another undamaged E-2 focusing screen sent to replace it. The other two focusing screens were in perfect condition.

Thank you.

I called to get return authorization this morning. Bob Kendall told me to send the focusing screen, along with a letter and a copy of the packing receipt (which I've enclosed), and he said the screen would be exchanged. Please send the new E-2 focusing screen as soon as possible. Thanks for your time.

Sincerely,

Nancy Powell

This letter is awkward, disjointed, and repetitive. The words "focusing screen" are repeated eight times! Also, the opening and closing are both weak and uninteresting. At our suggestion, Ms. Powell reorganized the letter to highlight the positive and make it easier to read:

May 11, 1993

Nancy Powell
9755 Afton St.
San Diego, CA 92117

Pete Hansen
Customer Service Manager
Triple C Camera
69 West 13th St.
New York, NY 10026

Dear Mr. Hansen:

Thank you for the prompt delivery of the three Nelson E-2 focusing screens I ordered on April 23, 1993. I received them on May 10, 1993.

Unfortunately, when I opened one of the boxes, I found that the focusing screen within had a large scratch on its bottom left corner. I am returning the damaged screen as I found it, and I would like another undamaged E-2 focusing screen sent in its place. The other two screens were in perfect condition.

I called to get return authorization this morning. Bob Kendall told me to return the damaged screen, along with a letter and a copy of the packing receipt, which I've enclosed. He said the screen would be exchanged and a new screen sent as soon as possible.

I appreciate this prompt and courteous service and look forward to doing more business with you.

Sincerely,

Nancy Powell

As you can see, the ideas have been more logically organized in this draft. The letter now emphasizes the positive aspects of the transaction by opening and closing on an upbeat, positive note. This letter invites a prompt, courteous response.

The look of the letter has also been improved by breaking up the text into smaller paragraphs, which adds white space and makes the letter easier to read. (See Chapter 7 for a fuller discussion of letter appearance.)

SUMMARY

There are, of course, exceptions to every rule. There are times when you may find it impossible to be positive. In these cases, it is important to remain businesslike and professional. State the facts clearly and concisely, avoiding anger, sarcasm, and emotionalism. Remember, the person to whom you are writing may not be the cause of the problem and may well be part of the solution. You want him or her on your side. At times you may also find it awkward to put your request at the very beginning of the letter. Again, that's a good rule, but not an absolute one. We've seen successful letters where the request is not put up front. Each situation is different, and each individual's writing style is unique. However, it is important to place the main point as *near* the beginning as possible. The first paragraph is best. Remember, the first and last paragraphs in a letter are the most powerful. Use them accordingly.

To sum up:

- *Decide beforehand what you want.*
- *Ask for it up front.*
- *Be specific. If you want money back, say how much.*
- *Be positive whenever possible.*
- *Be courteous and professional.*
- *Be reasonable and fair in your request.*
- *Be brief and get to your point quickly.*
- *End on a confident, positive note.*
- *Include copies of all necessary documents.*

In all but the most difficult cases, this formula will get the results you want. But what about those times when you are angry enough to throw a brick through a storefront window? How can you be positive and courteous when you'd rather knock someone's block off? That's the subject of our next chapter.

Taming the Roar of Your Tone

All of us have been angry at a company or service at one time or another. When you have been treated rudely, or a piece of merchandise has failed to work properly and the manufacturer doesn't seem to care, the last thing you want to do is be positive and courteous. You'd rather write an angry, nasty letter, telling the offending party exactly what you think of him or her.

Do it.

Get it off your chest. Write the angry letter.

Then set it aside and write the one you'll send.

Often you can think more clearly and rationally once you've given vent to your anger by writing it down. But sending that letter would be a mistake. Letters containing harsh criticism and juvenile expressions of anger put the recipient on the defensive. Put yourself in his or her shoes. How would you respond to a letter that was abusive and sarcastic? Probably not very favorably!

It bears repeating that if you follow our advice and write to the top, the person you are writing to is probably not directly responsible for your problem but is definitely part of the solution. You don't want to insult and anger that person—you want him or her on your side. Selecting a tone that is professional yet forceful guarantees that your complaint will be taken seriously.

CHOOSING THE RIGHT TONE

Your choice of tone is critical, and there are some important dos and don'ts to remember:

DO:

- *Be optimistic whenever possible.*

- *Use "thank you" where appropriate.*

- *Keep your tone conversational—avoid stuffy sounding words.*

- *Address the reader directly—use "you" in a friendly, non-accusatory way. Or use the reader's name.*

- *Use the active voice—avoid the passive.*

- *Be businesslike.*

DON'T:

- *Be brusque, abrasive, antagonistic, or sarcastic.*

- *Be syrupy and insincere.*

- *Use slang.*

- *Vent your anger and frustration.*

Venting your anger may feel good at the time, but will it get results? Chances are it won't. If you sound completely unreasonable in a letter, the recipient may decide it's better to lose you as a customer than it is to deal with you. Even if your letter does get results—if the president calls you up to apologize, or sends you a letter explaining why the problem occurred—you may end up feeling foolish for your outburst.

Worse, if you have to involve third parties such as attorneys or government agencies to get your complaint addressed, and they request a record of all your correspondence relating to the problem, it would be embarrassing to send them copies of your nasty letters. Those who might have supported you could wind

—— • ——

" I understand a fury in your words,
But not the words. "

—William Shakespeare
1564-1616

Othello

—— • ——

up being less than sympathetic to your cause. It is better to stick to the facts and avoid emotionalism.

Besides, the customer is always right. Right? Since you are the customer, you can afford to be professional and courteous. It's more likely you'll get results you want.

Test Market Your Tone

Once you've written the letter you want to send, test market the tone by giving it to someone you know and trust to read. That person will let you know if your tone is too harsh. Third parties can look at your complaint impartially; unlike yourself, they aren't emotionally connected to the situation.

One of our clients wrote the following letter to a mail-order camera store. She gave it to us to look at before sending it off:

May 21, 1993

Laura Gomez
8834 Fanuel St.
San Diego, CA 92109

General Manager
Tri-Star Camera Exchange
22 Third Ave.
New York, NY 10013

Dear General Manager:

I ordered a Nikkor AIS non-autofocus 28mm (2.8) lens, a lens case, and a 52mm L37C filter from your store on April 2, 1993. I have since received my Visa card statement, which shows that a transaction for $209.35 was made on April 12, 1993, for the above items ordered. So, you have my money. My question is this: Where is my photo equipment? It has been over 30 days since I ordered the stuff!

According to *Photography News,* "the advertiser (that's you) must ship the merchandise within 30 days after the receipt of a phone order (that's me). If an advertiser cannot ship the merchandise within the required delivery time, it must notify the customer (that's me again) by mail immediately of the revised shipping date. The reply card must give the customer the option of canceling the order or accepting the delay."

I know you guys in New York are very, very busy, but please give me just a little customer courtesy and let me know what's happening with my "merchandise" (and *please* don't tell me "the computers are down"). Thanks so very much for your precious time, and I look forward to hearing from you within 10 business days (otherwise, *Photography News* will just have to read this letter).

Sincerely,

Laura Gomez

An angry and sarcastic letter! Frankly, if we received a letter like this, our initial response would be anger and defensiveness. But we'd be inclined to ignore the letter rather than give in to our own anger and send a nasty reply.

We told Ms. Gomez that it was good she had written that letter and released her anger. Then we helped her write the letter she needed to send:

Laura Gomez   May 21, 1993
8834 Fanuel St.
San Diego, CA 92109

General Manager
Tri-Star Camera Exchange
22 Third Ave.
New York, NY 10013

Dear General Manager:
    It is important that I know the status of several items I ordered from your store last month. It has been over 30 days since I placed the order, yet I have not received the merchandise, nor have I received a revised shipping date from you.
    On April 2, 1993, I ordered a Nikkor AIS non-autofocus 28mm (2.8) lens, a lens case, and a 52mm L37C filter from your store. On April 17 I received a Visa card statement showing a transaction for $209.35, made on April 12, 1993, for the ordered items.
    As I'm sure you're aware, the *Photography News* policy concerning mail order advertising states, in part, "...the advertiser must ship the merchandise within 30 days after the receipt of a phone or mail order. If an advertiser cannot ship the merchandise within the required delivery time, it must notify the customer by mail immediately of the revised shipping date and must include a self-addressed, postage-paid reply card. The reply card must give the customer the option of canceling the order or accepting the delay."
    Please adhere to these guidelines. I have called twice for information, and your salespeople have rebuffed me each time. I will be traveling abroad next month, and it is critical that I know promptly the status of this equipment.
    Thank you.

Sincerely,

Laura Gomez

In this letter, it is still clear that the writer is angry and frustrated. However, the tone is more professional and unemotional. This letter is more likely to get the response Laura wants. In fact, her merchandise arrived shortly after she sent this letter.

So, before you send out your letter, test market the tone.

═══ ● ═══

" An old tutor of a college said to one of his pupils: Read over your compositions, and wherever you meet with a passage which you think is particularly fine, strike it out. "

—Samuel Johnson
1709-1784

═══ ● ═══

~~. . . I know you guys in New York are very, very busy, but please give me just a little customer courtesy and let me . . .~~

. . . Please adhere to these guidelines. I have called twice for information, and your salespeople have rebuffed me each time. I . . .

Be Angry But Not Offensive

As the previous rewrite demonstrates, it is fine to let your reader know you are angry—but do so without being insulting. One of our clients is the manager of a large hotel. When he learned we were writing this book, he dug through his files and produced the following letter.

March 15, 1993

John Forrester
768 Central Valley
Camden, IA 32695

Steve Patterson, Manager
Bay View Hotel
7344 Ocean Blvd.
Santa Barbara, CA 95773

Mr. Patterson:

We were guests in your hotel last week, and it was one of the worst experiences of our lives. I awoke in the middle of the night to the smell of smoke. When I opened our door and looked into the hallway, it was filled with smoke. I never heard any alarm! I woke my wife, and we made our way outside.

What kind of establishment are you running? Do you have no concern at all for your guests' lives? Why weren't the fire alarms working? We could have been killed, along with many other people. When we checked out, your clerk made no apology, nor would she have even mentioned the fire had we not brought it up. She seemed to think it was funny!

I think you are guilty of criminal neglect. We will never stay at your hotel again, and we will warn all of our friends. I am considering suing you and your company. As near as I can figure, you must be some kind of idiot, or else you don't care at all about the lives of your guests. If you did, you'd fix the fire alarms!

Disgusted,

John Forrester

The fire had actually been a minor one, restricted to a broom closet. No one had been injured, and there was only minor damage to the structure. Our client conceded that the smoke alarms should have sounded, and he was upset that they hadn't. He had them fixed immediately. Had he not been busy addressing the problem the next day, he would have been at the front counter personally apologizing to the guests.

Even though our client admitted that his company was at fault, he felt no compulsion to answer this insulting letter. Why should he? After all, Mr. Forrester had already made up his mind. He had shot off his letter without stopping to think that the hotel manager, rather than being at fault, might be just as angry and horrified as he was. Mr. Patterson stuck the letter in his files and ignored it, hoping Mr. Forrester would forget about it over time, which he apparently did.

But as an exercise, we rewrote the letter:

Dear Mr. Patterson:

I am very upset about our experience as guests of your hotel on March 8, 1993. As a result, I believe you should refund our money for that night. A copy of your bill for $95 is enclosed.

On that night, my wife and I awoke to the smell of smoke. We made our way quickly through the smoke-filled hallway to the stairwell and finally outside. At no time did we hear an alarm. When we checked out the next morning, there was no apology for the inconvenience, not to mention the threat to our lives and health.

I'm sure you realize the potential for tragedy in a situation like that. I strongly recommend that you investigate the status of your fire and smoke alarms, and that you ensure they will work in any future incidents. In the meantime, I will expect my check for $95.

Sincerely,

John Forrester

This letter is also angry, but it is businesslike and professional. It states the facts and makes a specific demand for reparation. We showed it to Mr. Patterson and asked him what his response would be. Without hesitation, he told us he would gladly refund the money and send it to Mr. Forrester with a letter of apology, along with an assurance that new alarms were being installed and the incident would never be repeated. It would be worth the effort, he said, to salvage Mr. Forrester's future business.

Be Firm But Not Threatening

If you have been wronged and you feel someone owes you a refund or an apology, or both, you need to be firm in your request. But making threats, though often tempting, is the wrong approach. When we threaten someone, we attempt to exercise some power over them. We are telling them that if they don't do what we want, they will suffer severe consequences. This is supposed to spur them to action.

In reality, threats have the opposite effect. Consider how you react when you are threatened. If you're like we are, you probably become indignant and defensive. The threats themselves may often seem childish and petulant. You may be tempted to respond with a cavalier, "Fine. Go ahead and do it. See if I care." Or you may simply decide to ignore the threat *and* the individual making it.

Empty threats are even worse than real threats. One writer opened his complaint letter with this phrase: "My father, an attorney, told me I shouldn't even bother writing you this letter."

Indeed, with an opening like that he certainly shouldn't have bothered writing. His implied threat was so obviously transparent and empty that the letter received no response. Most likely, the recipient got a good laugh out of it and tossed it into the garbage.

Our experience with complaint-letter writing is that making threats, empty or otherwise, is almost always counterproductive. We strongly advise against it. There are better, more efficient ways of getting your complaint addressed without creating defensiveness and bad feelings.

Read the following letter:

May 29, 1993

Margaret Kokes
Director of Customer Services
Cameo Videocable Service
P.O. Box 669
Portland, OR 97226

RE: Account #99673

Dear Ms. Kokes:

Because your delivery of premium and regular channels is far below normal and acceptable standards, I hope to petition the Federal Communications Commission to revoke your franchise for Ines County.

I have been paying dearly for a subscription service, and it is the generally accepted business practice of a subscription commodity not to charge for nondelivery.

Not one week has gone by without major service interruptions or nondelivery. Last evening we had the opportunity to view all of about four channels. I could do better with an antenna.

I'm paying more than $650 annually, and what I'm paying for is enhanced signal delivery and entertainment channels. I'm not receiving either consistently.

If service does not improve significantly, I will cancel my service. I shall also petition the FCC for a rebate on nondelivered subscription service. Every time I call your Bakersfield office, I'm told, "We have a problem in Valley Park, but we're working on it." It seems you've been working on it for about three years now.

Disappointedly,

Ron Miller
995 Midway
Valley Park, CA 93775

cc: FCC
Dept. of Consumer Affairs
Better Business Bureau

If we were the executives of that cable company, and this was the first letter we had received from Mr. Miller, we would be angry and defensive. Why hadn't he written before if he had been unhappy for so long? Why did he have to start the letter with a threat, and probably an empty one at that. It would take time and effort to place a petition before the FCC, and we doubt Mr. Miller would bother.

This letter makes threats but asks for no specific action except a vague "improvement of service." Our reaction would be either to ignore it, or terminate the account ourselves and refund Mr. Miller's money. Good riddance.

Here's how we would address the problem:

Dear Ms. Kokes:

I'm very unhappy with the service I have received from your company. I would like your personal guarantee that I will be receiving all of the fifteen channels I am paying for—and consistently—by June 12, 1993. If this is not possible, I wish to have my fees for January through May, 1993, a total of $285, refunded in full.

For the past three years I have paid for enhanced reception and entertainment channels, neither of which I have received consistently. Last night I was able to view only four channels. I'm certain I could do better with an antenna. Each time I call your office, I'm told, "There is a problem, but we're working on it."

That is not acceptable. Please let me know if you will be able to provide the service you promise. Otherwise, cancel my account and refund my money so that I may take my business elsewhere.

Thank you. I look forward to hearing from you by June 12.

Sincerely,

Ron Miller

This less threatening letter would probably get a desirable response—probably a refund, since it doesn't seem likely that improved reception will happen any time soon. If the company balks at giving a refund, then it's time to write a stronger letter and notify the appropriate agencies. The point here is this: if it ever becomes necessary or desirable to bring in third parties, don't threaten—just do it. We'll cover the involvement of third parties more extensively in Chapter 9.

SUMMARY

Remember the importance of keeping anger, sarcasm, and petulance out of your letter. People respond most favorably to positive, professional, businesslike letters. If you need to get the anger out of your system, write a nasty letter—then throw it away and write the one you should send. In a nutshell:

- *Choose an appropriate tone.*
- *Test market your tone.*
- *Be angry but not offensive.*
- *Be firm but not threatening.*

By sticking to the facts and avoiding emotion, your letters will get you the results you want—without creating ill will. That's what a successful complaint letter is all about.

The Look
of the Letter

First impressions are important. This is particularly true when it comes to correspondence. Most people first judge a letter by the way it looks rather than by what it says. That's why it's crucial to pay attention to the overall appearance of your letter, as well as to its content.

In the last few chapters we have shown you what to say and how to say it. In this chapter we will explain how to make your message look professional and, most important, readable.

FIRST IMPRESSIONS

There are several simple rules to follow to guarantee that your letter will get the attention it deserves. Some of these rules are straightforward; others are less obvious but are just as critical. We'll take them one at a time.

Handwritten Versus Typewritten

This rule is first and foremost. Complaint letters, or any other kind of business letters, should always be typewritten (or printed with a quality printer if you use a word processor). There are no exceptions to this rule. Handwritten letters lack credibility. They are fine for your thank-you note to Aunt Esther, or when you are writing to a good friend. In the business world, however, handwritten letters don't look professional. They are simply not acceptable. If you want your complaint letter to be taken seriously, use a typewriter or word processor.

Appropriate Paper

When erasable bond typewriter papers first came on the market, they were a blessing. The days of retyping whole pages to correct a single error were over. However, anyone who has ever used erasable bond knows that the blessing is mixed. The paper is sticky and tends to curl. It is, in fact, very unpleasant to deal with. And, in these days of self-correcting typewriters and word processors, erasable bond is entirely unnecessary.

Most professional writers, teachers, and editors avoid using erasable typewriter paper. Some of those same editors and teachers even refuse to accept manuscripts typed on such paper. We recommend that you avoid using it.

Stay away, too, from onionskin, linen, colored, or other specialty papers. (The last thing you want is for your letter to look like a high school project.) The purpose of the paper is not to call attention to itself. We recommend that you use plain, white, 20-pound typing paper for all correspondence. Or, if you use a word processor, standard 20-pound perforated or single-sheet computer paper is acceptable.

The only exception we make is in the case of letterhead. If you own or are associated with a company that uses letterhead paper, it is often a good idea to use that for your complaint letter. Appearances are important in this world, after all. Using letterhead paper can give you that extra bit of credibility.

Format

There are many different ways to format a business letter; most of them are equally acceptable in the business community. Some people place the date in the upper right area of the first page; others put it in the upper left. Some indent the first line of each paragraph with no space between paragraphs; others use block style for paragraphs and separate them with a line space.

We won't go into the particulars of letter format here. The

bibliography contains a list of style, grammar, and format books that treat this subject in great detail. We refer you to them for explanations of the many generally acceptable formats.

The trend in the business world today, however, is toward a standardized format. This is a left-justified, right-ragged block format, and it is the one we prefer and recommend. On non-letterhead paper it looks like this:

Month Day, Year

Your Name
Address
City, State ZIP

Addressee Name
Title or Position
Company Name
Address
City, State ZIP

Salutation (Dear Mr./Ms.):

First paragraph.

Subsequent paragraphs.

Sincerely,

Your Name

Enclosures (if necessary)

cc: (if necessary)

This format follows the formula 4, 2, 2, 1, 1, 2, 4: 4 spaces between the date and your name and address, 2 spaces between your name and address and that of your recipient, 2 spaces between your recipient's address and the salutation, 1 space between the salutation and the body of the letter, 1 space between paragraphs, 2 spaces between the last paragraph and the sign-off, and 4 spaces between the sign-off and your name (this leaves room for you to sign your name above the printed version). If an enclosure line is necessary, it follows 2 lines after your name. If a cc line is necessary, it follows 2 lines after the enclosure line.

This format is becoming standard. It's easy to work with and easy to read. We recommend it for all complaint letters. (See Appendix A for examples.)

If you are using letterhead paper, the format remains essentially the same except that you go directly from the date line to the recipient's name and address (separated by 4 lines). The letterhead serves as your return address, and the only time your name appears is in the signature line at the end.

Length

We've mentioned this before, but it bears repeating: Keep your letter to one page if possible. The people you are writing to are very busy. Multiple-page letters take too long to read, especially if they don't come to the point quickly. If you have too much information for one page, try to provide as much of it as possible in attachments. Supply copies of receipts and transactions. These dated papers will provide the necessary facts; you need only sum up your problem.

If your problem is complicated and covers a long period of time, consider drafting a point-by-point synopsis and sending it as an attachment. Then you can summarize your complaint in your letter, providing just enough information to make your case clear. If your reader wants the details, he or she can find them easily in your synopsis.

The rule on length: Be clear and concise.

Proper margins

Margins should be one inch on all four sides: top, bottom, left, and right. Adequate margins help your letter "breathe." It looks better and is more inviting. When text goes from edge to edge and top to bottom, the letter looks cluttered and imposing.

White space

Proper use of white space is perhaps the least known but one of the most important aspects of letter appearance. If your high school English classes were like ours, you weren't told about white space. If anything, you were encouraged to fill your papers up with words.

But that is exactly the wrong thing to do in a complaint letter. Letters that look like massive, undifferentiated blocks of words turn your readers off. Like adequate margins, white space lets your letter breathe and makes it look inviting and readable. And that, of course, is what you want.

Look at the following example:

April 24, 1994

Henry Jansen
1227 Toreno Place
Corpus Christi, TX 76553

Peter Epstein
President
Tandell Optics, Co.
23 Lakeview Terrace
Dayton, OH 32665

Dear Mr. Epstein:

    I am having trouble getting a pair of Tandell binoculars repaired by your factory. I want to bring this to your attention. I have owned this pair of binoculars for several years and have been very happy with them. Recently they went out of adjustment, so I sent them in for repair. Yesterday the binoculars were returned, with a note saying they could not be repaired because they were obsolete. Your statement is difficult to accept. How can a pair of perfectly good binoculars be obsolete? I am dismayed by your lack of faith in your product. At this point, I would think twice before buying another Tandell product. Please address this problem. I'm certain some way can be found to repair my binoculars so that they can serve me again.

    I look forward to hearing from you.

Sincerely,

Henry Jansen

    What an imposing mess! When we receive a letter like this, it goes to the bottom of the pile. And this letter is only one page long! Imagine the same condensed prose continuing for two, three, or even four pages! We've seen letters like that, but who has time to struggle through them? We don't, and certainly not a busy company president.

Let's add some white space to that letter to make it look more readable:

April 24, 1994

Henry Jansen
1227 Toreno Place
Corpus Christi, TX 76553

Peter Epstein
President
Tandell Optics Co.
23 Lakeview Terrace
Dayton, OH 32665

Dear Mr. Epstein:

I am having trouble getting a pair of Tandell binoculars repaired by your factory. I want to bring this to your attention.

I have owned this pair of binoculars for several years and have been very happy with them. Recently they went out of adjustment, so I sent them in for repair. Yesterday the binoculars were returned, with a note saying they could not be repaired because they were obsolete.

Your statement is difficult to accept. How can a pair of perfectly good binoculars be obsolete? I am dismayed by your lack of faith in your product. At this point, I would think twice before buying another Tandell product.

Please address this problem. I'm certain some way can be found to repair my binoculars so that they can serve me again.

I look forward to hearing from you.

Sincerely,

Henry Jansen

Which letter would you rather receive? Which letter are you more likely to read? Obviously, the second version is the clear winner. Both letters contain the same number of words, but the second version is certainly the more readable of the two. That's the benefit of adequate white space, and the effect you want to produce in your own complaint letters.

SUMMARY

Make your complaint letters readable and accessible by using:

- *A typewriter or word processor*
- *Appropriate paper*
- *Adequate margins*
- *Proper format*
- *Adequate white space.*

And don't overwrite. Keep your letter brief. If it looks inviting and easy to read, it's more likely to be read, and therefore get you the results you want.

When You Don't Get What You Want/ When You *Do* Get What You Want

In our experience, a well-written, well-directed complaint letter will be successful in most situations. However, there may be times when your first letter gets a response but the result is not the one you wanted.

WHEN YOU DON'T GET WHAT YOU WANT

Rirst and foremost: Don't give up. We've talked about this before: Your first letter is really only the first shot out of your arsenal. Sometimes you will have to write two, three, or even more letters before the offending party sees things your way.

Strengthen Your Tone

The key to making this multiletter approach work is knowing how to strengthen your tone appropriately. Your first letter should be as courteous as possible given the circumstances. If it doesn't get your problem solved, you need to take a slightly different approach. Strengthening your tone doesn't mean becoming emotional or insulting. It simply means adopting a no-nonsense tone that lets the reader know that you are not happy with the situation and won't give up until a satisfactory solution is reached. Period.

There's a story that illustrates the point. A young boy wanted to borrow his older brother's baseball mitt. First he asked nicely, "Can I please borrow your baseball mitt?" When the older brother refused, the younger strengthened his tone, "Come on, let me use your mitt." When that still didn't work, the resourceful young fellow beefed up his request even more: "Let me use your mitt or I'll tell Dad about the time you took five dollars out of his wallet."

He got the baseball mitt.

Of course, we don't recommend threats and extortion! Nonetheless, there is a two-fold message here: First, by strengthening his tone in successive requests, the younger brother made it clear that he was not about to give up. Second, he knew when to bring in the threat of a powerful third party. In a complaint letter, that would be the "cc."

Strengthen Your Case

Some professionals feel that all you need to do is place a "cc" line at the bottom of your letter and list the appropriate agencies and individuals. They never actually send copies to those agencies, but rather rely upon the letter recipient's belief that the copies were sent, to prod him or her to action.

Others do send copies to the people listed, but with no accompanying cover letter.

The third method is to involve the third parties fully by sending a copy *and* an explanatory cover letter. This is the procedure we prefer, though if you want to save yourself effort, you might consider holding off on the copies for 10 days to see if your "cc" works. If it doesn't, and you still get no response, then go ahead and send out the copies—along with brief, accompanying cover letters.

The following is an example of a cover letter we might send along with a "cc":

February 15, 1994

Walter Montcreaf
Fraud Division
Santa Cruz County District Attorney
884 Riverside
Santa Cruz, CA 96068

Dear Mr. Montcreaf:

The enclosed photocopies will let you know I am having a problem with the Halogen Co. They have consistently refused to respond to my letters and phone calls. Meanwhile, I am out $500 for defective lamps.

I wonder if this company has a history of reneging on warranties? I'd appreciate any information or assistance you could give me.

Thank you.

Sincerely,

Allen T. Yarstrow

Enclosures: Photocopied correspondence

Be sure to include copies of all previous correspondence between you and the company or individual causing your problem.

Generally, once the problem has been expanded to include others, particularly regulatory and law-enforcement agencies, the offending party will decide that it's better to give you what you want rather than deal with what could become a much larger problem. A key factor in this approach, as in the story of the two brothers, is their realization that you are not going to give up until you get a fair resolution to the problem.

We can't stress this enough. Most complaint-letter writers will conclude that they have failed if their first attempt doesn't get the desired response. Either that or they decide the problem is no longer worth any more of their effort. They swallow their pride, bid their money adieu, and chalk up the experience to another of life's hard lessons. We hear this time and time again.

It is absolutely wrong!

Don't give up! If your first letter doesn't succeed, your second or third will. Don't give up! If the company or persons you are complaining to think they can outwait you and save themselves the trouble of addressing your problem, they'll do it. Don't give up!

The following series of letters illustrates our point.

April 10, 1993

Janet Attinger
1384 Socorro
Tucson, AZ 88456

Allan Pencader, President
Larson Corporation
584-3 Toulane Road
Cleveland, OH 35997

Dear Mr. Pencader:

I am writing to ask for your help in solving a problem with my Larson microwave oven. When I called your service department on June 2, 1992, they directed me to Visco Appliances, which is your authorized repair agent in this area. Their response has not been satisfactory.

My Larson Cookmaster microwave began rusting before the one-year warranty was up. When I took it to Visco for repair under warranty, they told me "tough." They were either unable or unwilling to help. A friend told me about Marten Appliance, a Larson factory representative in Tucson. When I contacted them they were most helpful. They said they could repair the oven, but that the cost would be about $175.

My question is this: Will Larson trust my word that the rusting occurred before the warranty period was up and cover the price of repair? I shopped around for months before I decided, through *Consumer Reports*, friends, and other sources, that Larson was a name to be trusted. Some of my friends bought less expensive microwaves and theirs are still fine. They are giving me a pretty hard time about buying a "name brand."

I bought the microwave at Branigan's Furniture on March 23, 1992. The serial number is 63395, model number 201. Peter Branigan, the owner of the furniture store, thinks very highly of Larson products. I have bought appliances from him for 18 years and have never gone wrong. I love the microwave and would hate being without it. Since I work full-time and have three teenaged sons, the microwave makes my life much easier.

Please let me hear from you regarding this unfortunate situation.

Sincerely,

Janet Attinger

The first response, on Larson letterhead, was less than satisfactory:

April 28, 1993

Janet Attinger
1384 Socorro
Tucson, AZ 88456

Dear Ms. Attinger:

Thank you for contacting Larson Microwave Cooking Products.

I was most sorry to hear about the problem that you have encountered with one of our products.

Because we want to react to your complaint in a manner that is fair to you, it will be necessary for you to supply us with the following information: a copy of your bill of sale for your microwave oven and copies of all service invoices for repairs made on your unit.

Upon receipt of this information, your complete file will be reviewed.

Sincerely,

Marian Bromowski
Customer Service
Larson Microwave
Cooking Products

Mr. Pencader obviously did not want to deal with Janet Attinger's letter and shuffled it off to a lower-level customer service representative. Nonetheless, Ms. Attinger sent the requested information (which actually should have been included with her first letter). Nothing happened. Two weeks later, she wrote again:

May 15, 1993

Marian Bromowski
Customer Service
Larson Corporation
584-3 Toulane Road
Cleveland, OH 35997

Dear Ms. Bromowski:

On April 30, I sent you the information you requested concerning my Larson microwave oven. I have not heard from you since. The oven is continuing to rust, and a hole is beginning to develop that may be irreparable if left for much longer.

Please let me know what you intend to do about this problem as soon as possible.

Sincerely,

Janet Attinger

This second letter got a response, but not the one she wanted.

June 2, 1993

Janet Attinger
1384 Socorro
Tucson, AZ 88456

Dear Ms. Attinger:

Thank you for contacting Larson Microwave Cooking Products.

We are sorry to hear that it will be necessary for you to have repairs made to your Larson oven.

An authorized service agent would be able to sand the rusted area and apply new paint, or in extreme cases replace the cavity. The cost of this repair would be at your expense.

If you need assistance in locating an authorized service agency, please contact our Customer Service Department at 800-455-9947.

We appreciate hearing from you and are sure you will continue to enjoy many more years of microwave cooking.

Sincerely,

Marian Bromowski
Customer Service
Larson Microwave
Cooking Products

This is about as weak and unsatisfactory a response as Janet could imagine. The tone is ingratiating, and it is apparent that Ms. Bromowski had completely forgotten about Janet Attinger's complaint—either that or she had set it aside to be forgotten. In this case, "customer service" is anything but.

═══ ● ═══

" For the service interaction to be successful for both parties over the long term, both the service provider and the customer must feel that they each won. Customers must feel they received the service they expected at a price they accept. And the service provider must also feel good about providing the service— and that includes making a profit on the transaction. The win-win approach is the new paradigm that works as the model for customer service. "

—Fred E. Jandt

The Customer Is Usually Wrong!

═══ ● ═══

Ms. Attinger fired off her third letter immediately, straight to the president of the company:

June 8, 1993

Janet Attinger
1384 Socorro
Tucson, AZ 88456

Allan Pencader, President
Larson Corporation
584-3 Toulane Road
Cleveland, OH 35997

Dear Mr. Pencader:

I am writing to you to express my disappointment in your product and your company. I have enclosed correspondence between your ineffective Customer Service Department and myself, which is self-explanatory. I am asking you to direct your attention toward finding a solution.

Marten Appliance is making the necessary repairs to my microwave, at a cost of $175. I paid $270 for it only a year and a half ago. I am very sorry I bought a Larson. A friend of mine bought a less expensive microwave a full year before I bought this one, and his is doing fine. I'm embarrassed that I had to have the best—which I thought was Larson!

At this point, I would never recommend a Larson to anyone. In fact, I intend to show my correspondence and explain the problems I have encountered to anyone I meet who is contemplating buying a microwave. This will include Peter Branigan, the owner of Branigan's Appliance where I made this purchase. Furthermore, I'm sure *Consumer Reports* will be interested.

I feel I have not been treated fairly. I obviously bought a "lemon," and your company has refused to do anything about it. You must not believe in your own products. Your company is a great disappointment to me.

Sincerely,

Janet Attinger

Enclosures
cc: Peter Branigan
Consumer Reports
Better Business Bureau
Major Appliance Consumer Action Panel

Notice how the tone of this letter is significantly more forceful than in the first letter she sent. The language is stronger without being emotional or abusive.

Here is an example of the cover letter she sent out along with the "cc's":

June 8, 1993

Janet Attinger
1384 Socorro
Tucson, AZ 88456

Consumer Reports
Consumer's Union of U.S., Inc.
256 Washington Street
Mount Vernon, NY 10553

Dear Consumer Reports:

I am having a problem with Larson Microwave. The enclosed copies of my correspondence with them will explain the situation in detail. Essentially, I have found a product to be defective, but Larson's management refuses to honor their warranty.

Because you have consistently listed Larson high on your list of quality, I thought you would be interested. Can you help me to resolve this problem? Have you had any other complaints about them?

I look forward to hearing from you.

Sincerely,

Janet Attinger

Enclosures
cc: Allan Pencader
Larson Microwave

Here's the response she received from Larson a few days later:

June 20, 1993

Janet Attinger
1384 Socorro
Tucson, AZ 88456

Dear Ms. Attinger:

Thank you for contacting Larson Microwave Cooking Products in regards to your model 201 oven.

We have received your most recent letter and have again reviewed all of the facts in your case.

If you would please send in your itemized bill for the repair, we will reimburse you for the cost of the parts.

Your immediate reply will assist in processing your claim.

Sincerely,

Marian Bromowski
Customer Service
Larson Microwave
Cooking Products

This time Mr. Pencader apparently gave the Customer Service Department a different set of directions. Perhaps one of the facts they reviewed was that Janet Attinger was not going to give up! Whether it was that or her introduction of third parties that tipped the scale in her favor, we don't know. It doesn't matter. The point is that perseverance got results.

Ms. Attinger mailed a copy of the itemized bill and received this letter a few days later:

July 10, 1993

Janet Attinger
1384 Socorro
Tucson, AZ 88456

Dear Ms. Attinger:

Thank you for your letter concerning your Larson microwave oven.

Your service history has been reviewed. We are pleased to inform you that authorization has been given to reimburse you for parts.

A check in the amount of $150.86 will arrive under separate cover. Please allow 3 weeks for processing and delivery.

We appreciate your taking the time to advise us of your situation. We are confident that your unit is operating properly and that you are again enjoying the advantages of microwave cooking.

Sincerely,

Marian Bromowski
Customer Service
Larson Microwave
Cooking Products

We reproduced this final letter from Larson to point out a few things. Throughout the entire process, Ms. Bromowski's tone never changed to reflect her familiarity with Ms. Attinger's problem. Even in this final letter, her style is stilted, overly formal, and insincere.

" The development of good communication skills is essential to your success in life. You can't escape communicating with those around you. Whether you speak or not, you are sending messages to everyone you meet. The opinions others have about you are formed by the way you communicate. If you are able to express your ideas to others, they will see you in a positive way. "

—Marsha Ludden

Effective Communication Skills

These are things you should avoid in your own writing. It doesn't do you any good and may even hinder your attempts to get your problem solved if you sound like an impersonal robot in your letter. Certainly, as you can see here, it did nothing for our opinion of Ms. Bromowski's dedication to her corporate function, let alone Larson's corporate image.

When you must turn up the heat in your own letters, follow Janet Attinger's example. Be direct. Avoid passive expressions ("authorization has been given") and empty phrases ("thank you for contacting Larson...").

Starting a letter with "thank you" is generally acceptable. However, in this case it's obviously a "stock" phrase plugged into a form letter. It clearly sounds insincere and forced. That's the type of thing you want to avoid.

The style of business communication is changing. Less formal, more direct, and more sincere letters are becoming the standard. They are easier to write and more positively received.

WHEN YOU DO GET WHAT YOU WANT

Two weeks later, Janet Attinger received her check from Larson. She used the opportunity to transform her experience into a positive one and develop a better relationship with the company:

July 28, 1993

Janet Attinger
1384 Socorro
Tucson, AZ 88456

Allan Pencader
President
Larson Corporation
584-3 Toulane Road
Cleveland, OH 35997

Dear Mr. Pencader:

Thank you for reconsidering my case regarding the Larson microwave. I now believe that you are standing behind your product, and that makes me feel better about buying future Larson products. Friends who have been following this problem also feel more positive toward Larson.

You have restored my faith in brand names. I have always felt that when you buy a good, brand name product, you are also purchasing the company's "pride-in-product." I'm happy that Larson feels that pride.

Sincerely,

Janet Attinger

By taking this extra effort, Janet Attinger turned a negative situation into a positive one. While it was clear that people at the Larson Corporation would already remember her, she made certain that the company would remember her in a positive way. She can be assured that, if she has any further difficulties with Larson products, her next complaint will be addressed quickly and satisfactorily.

We recommend this procedure. Once your complaint has been dealt with to your satisfaction, take the time to write a follow-up letter, thereby building a good, positive working relationship with the company or individual. The effort required is minimal, but the potential benefits are great. You become a valuable voice not only for yourself but also for other consumers. You know that the company will listen to you, and that you can buy their products with confidence.

CHAPTER

9

When Writing
Doesn't Work

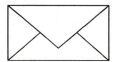

Let's say you gave it your best shot. You wrote a powerful, well-stated letter and received no response. You followed up with a second, stronger note and sent copies to the appropriate agencies, and still you've heard nothing. What now?

Your arsenal is far from exhausted. Now is the time to bring in the third parties we mentioned briefly in previous chapters. There are several agencies and organizations, public and private, that can help you resolve a complaint. Some resources, such as district attorneys and state attorney generals, are geared toward law enforcement but have consumer protection divisions. Others, like Consumers Union and media programs, focus on consumer activism. Still others, like trade associations and the Better Business Bureau, are private industry groups with the capacity to mediate disputes.

All these are legitimate avenues for help, but the ones you choose to contact will depend on the nature of your complaint and the type of business causing your problem. We'll discuss this in more detail later in the chapter. First, though, we need to talk about records and research.

RECORDS

Your efforts to engage the help of a third party may be futile if you don't have convincing proof of your claim. You may say you called the offending company three times and wrote two letters, but if you didn't keep a record of the calls and copies of the letters, your words have little meaning. There is no proof.

That's why it's critically important to *keep all records*. Each time you make a phone call to anyone connected with your complaint, write down the day and time of the call. Whenever possible, find out the name of the person you spoke to. This is particularly vital. A trail of names gives you a great deal of credibility. It would be difficult for a company to deny you had called when you can present a list of people you spoke to.

Finally, after each call jot down the result: what the person you spoke to said, what action would be taken on your behalf, if any, and the like. Keep a chronological list of these calls.

The same goes for correspondence. Whenever you write to an individual or company concerning a complaint, keep a copy of the letter in a file. This includes letters to agencies and organizations, as well as to the offending party. In the same file, keep all receipts, service records, and warranties. When you must send this information to someone, such as a customer service department or a state agency, *send only photocopies. Keep all originals.*

Keeping full and accurate documentation of your complaint strengthens your position significantly, especially if it becomes necessary for you to call in outside help. The third party you contact will see at a glance that you are well-organized and businesslike. That perception gives you immediate credibility. Also, if a full record of your complaint is available for study, it saves everyone time and effort in trying to track down the sequence of events.

To repeat: *Keep all records.*

RESEARCH

Before you contact a third party for assistance, and sometimes even before you write your first letter to the offending company or individual, it's a good idea to do some research. It is to your advantage to find out a little about the company or service you are dealing with.

For instance, has this company or individual been the subject of other recent complaints? A quick call to the district attorney's office will give you the answer. Have you been subjected to common trade practices? Is the price you paid for the service or item a fair one? A few calls to other businesses offering the same service or products will answer those questions.

In fact, it's a good idea to find out as much as you can about the business—its pricing structure and techniques, for instance—before you write. This is particularly applicable with service-oriented firms like construction contractors, physicians, and attorneys. The more you know, the stronger your bargaining position, and the less easily the wool can be pulled over your eyes.

Find out the offending company's weaknesses and its assets. If the company or individual must be licensed by the state to practice, as contractors are, make sure you get the state license number. In the case of contractors, three complaints against a license in California can lead to the license being revoked. This kind of information can be very valuable.

It is also advisable to investigate strange claims. Don Nagle, the president of Charandon Advertising in California and an adept complaint-letter writer, relates this story:

Once while Don was having a pool installed, the contractor stopped work with the claim that Environmental Protection Agency regulations prohibited work until a certain water problem was cleared up. A phone call by Nagle to the EPA unmasked this as a fraudulent, spurious attempt to delay a promised completion date.

CHOOSING APPROPRIATE THIRD PARTIES

Once you are ready to call for help, you must first decide whom to contact. Deciding that can sometimes be difficult, only because there are so many possibilities. Your best bet is to approach the agencies or organizations with the most influence over the offending company. The U.S. Office of Consumer Affairs publishes a handbook entitled the *Consumer's Resource Handbook,* which offers a reasonably comprehensive listing of these agencies and organizations. This handbook is free. Write to the Consumer Information Center in Pueblo, Colorado, 81009, or call 719-948-3334. It's updated every two years. In our experience, it's a valuable resource.

There are essentially four types of "third party" organizations: trade associations; consumer advocate groups; the media; and local, state, and federal government agencies. We'll discuss each one in turn.

Trade Associations

There are almost 40,000 trade associations in the United States, representing nearly every type of manufacturing or service business—everything from banks, clothing manufacturers, insurance companies, and automobile dealers to lawyers, doctors, and physical therapists. Examples would be the Photo Marketing Association, the American Hotel and Motel Association, or the Major Appliance Consumer Action Panel. You can find a complete listing of these organizations in a publication entitled the *National Trade and Professional Associations of the United States,* available at your local public library. There is also a brief list in the back of the *Consumer's Resource Handbook* that we mentioned.

What's the advantage of going to a trade association for help? These organizations are concerned with the public perception of their business. If one member of the association is engaging in undesirable or even unscrupulous practices, the other members have a great interest in setting things straight.

Why should they allow one bad company to be a reflection on all the member companies?

For instance, automobile repair shops have historically had to deal with a bad public image. Their association would be particularly sensitive to charges that one shop was charging for new parts and installing old ones. They would exert considerable influence on the malefactor not only to address your complaint, but also to cease the illegal activities or face expulsion and even prosecution.

Also, trade associations frequently have dispute resolution programs set up to handle complaints. Before engaging their services, you should check to see what the rules are. In some cases, the decision of the mediators is binding on all parties, in others it is binding only on the company, and in some the decision is not binding on either party.

Better Business Bureaus (BBB) are often included in a discussion of trade associations. These are organizations set up by local businesses to provide information and sometimes handle complaints. However, we have excluded them here for a very simple reason: We have never found them to be very helpful. In San Diego, where we live, we have never once been able to get through to the BBB for information or help. The situation may be different where you live, so it's worth trying. A list of the Better Business Bureaus for each state appears in Appendix B.

Consumer Advocate Groups

Everyone is familiar with the name Ralph Nader, the man who is perhaps the most famous consumer advocate in the world. Most major cities have a branch of the Public Interest Research Group, which he founded over two decades ago (1970). Since its inception, this group has had a profound effect on the way businesses operate in this country. Much of PIRG's effort has been directed toward investigating unsafe products and unscrupulous business practices. If your complaint falls into one of these categories, this group may be able to provide some assistance. You can find the branch of the Public Interest Research Group for your area in the phone book.

Another important group is Consumers Union (CU), which publishes the magazines *Consumer Reports* and *Consumers Union News Digest.* The focus here is on seeking safety, quality, and competitive pricing in consumer merchandise. Consumers Union actively invites direct consumer input. If you've purchased an inferior item that the manufacturer refuses to stand behind, CU would be interested. They may initiate an investigation into the product or company on the basis of your complaint. You can obtain more information by purchasing a copy of *Consumer Reports* at your local newsstand, or by writing to Consumers Union, 256 Washington St., Mt. Vernon, NY 10553.

The advantage in contacting these groups directly is less for what they can do for you personally than for the pressure they can exert on the offending party. Both groups have broad access to the media and to the public. If the owner of the company you are complaining about knows that a company product is going to be displayed in an unfavorable light, either in a magazine or in a press release, he or she may become instantly more willing to address your complaint.

The Media

Many local radio and television stations, and even some newspapers, have instituted consumer action hot lines for addressing problems and complaints. Most of these address only local complaints and so may not be useful for a problem involving a large, national company. However, on the local level these "hot lines" exert considerable leverage. As we said earlier, no company or service wants its name plastered across the newspaper or blasted over the airwaves in an unfavorable manner. When faced with that prospect, most businesses and professionals will go out of their way to solve your problem— before it goes public.

Contact your local newspapers, radio stations, and television stations to see if they supply these services, and how you can use them.

Government Agencies

Government is divided into three levels: local, state, and federal. Each one has agencies for addressing consumer complaints.

Local. On this level, the most appropriate agency for dealing with a complaint is the district attorney. There is usually a fraud division that handles complaints and keeps track of the number of complaints against companies in the attorney's jurisdiction. If a product or service has been misrepresented, and you can get no satisfaction from the company or individual responsible, the district attorney is the person to contact. You'll find the individual's number, and that of the fraud division, in your telephone directory's government pages.

State. There are several state agencies you can approach for help in solving a problem. One of the most useful and effective is the Office of the State Attorney General. Most state attorney general offices have a consumer rights or consumer protection division designed to investigate and, where possible, resolve consumer complaints. You'll also find this number in the government section of your telephone book.

A woman we know purchased a video camera by mail a few months ago, but did not receive it on the designated date. After several phone calls to the supplier and two complaint letters, none of which received a response, she contacted the attorney general's office in Texas, where the company was located. An investigation followed, and the operation turned out to be shady. Although the woman never received a camera or a refund, she at least had the satisfaction of knowing that the "con men" running the operation were prosecuted.

In less severe cases your initial letter to the attorney

general, with a copy sent to the offending party, will probably get your problem solved. No company wants government intervention and will likely move quickly to meet your demands.

It may also be useful to contact the state occupational or professional licensing board that issued an operating license to the source of your complaint. There are over 1,500 such agencies across the nation. They license or register more than 550 professions and service industries. These include accountants, doctors, lawyers, pharmacists, plumbers, electricians, auto repair shops, and many others.

The agencies set operating and licensing standards and rules and regulations, and can bring disciplinary action. They may even revoke licenses in severe cases. Many licensing agencies have divisions set up to handle consumer complaints directly. To locate the office nearest you, check the state government section of your telephone directory. You can also contact the state consumer protection division of the attorney general's office for information.

All states also maintain separate agencies for the regulation and overseeing of banking, insurance, and utilities. If your complaint involves one of these businesses, contact the appropriate authority. Again, the number can be found in the phone book or by calling the state consumer protection office.

A list of these government agencies—local, state, and federal-can be obtained from the U.S. Office of Consumer Affairs.

Federal. There are many federal agencies with jurisdiction over consumer complaints and inquiries—far too many to list here. Each agency has its own area of jurisdiction, though there may be some degree of overlap between two or more. For help in identifying which agency is best suited to deal with your complaint, contact your nearest federal information center.

As an example, one very useful source of help is the postal inspector. If you're experiencing a problem with mail order, or if you suspect you may have been the subject of mail order fraud, the postal inspector's office is the place to go for help. Write and explain the problem, and send a copy of your letter to the offending party.

Whom Do You Choose?

With so many resources to choose from, whom do you go to first? Each complaint and each situation is different and requires its own approach. Nonetheless, a few guidelines are useful.

We believe it is usually better to work with market forces and organizations first—trade associations and consumer advocate groups. These organizations do have clout and can be very helpful. If these organizations aren't available or appropriate, or if they can't make any headway with your problem, we recommend turning to government and law-enforcement agencies.

However, if you feel a law has been broken or the operation you are complaining about is shady and suspicious, we recommend going to the authorities first. Ultimately, though, you'll have to decide which third party can best serve your needs for your particular situation.

WRITING TO A THIRD PARTY

When writing to a third party, it is important to abide by a few rules. First of all, most private and public consumer-aid agencies insist that you attempt to solve your complaint yourself before seeking their help. If you have not done everything reasonably possible, they may refuse to help you until you have. Never go to them until you have written to the offending party on your own.

Second, be sure to include copies of *all* documents and correspondence between you and the company or individual to whom you are complaining. Also include a chronological record of any phone calls.

Third, keep your letter brief, to the point, and unemotional. Stick to the facts, and let your copies and other documents tell the story.

Be sure to send a copy of any correspondence between you and an agency back to the offending party, to remind them that you do not intend to let the matter drop until a satisfactory agreement is reached. This alone may be all it takes to get a resolution of your complaint.

On the following page is an example of what a letter to an agency might look like.

May 25, 1993

John Doe
77463 Consumer Road
Anytown, TX 77777

Joe Smith
Commissioner
State Contractor's Licensing Board
533 Capitol Street
Houston, TX 77565

Dear Commissioner Smith:

You will see from the enclosed correspondence that I have been having a great deal of trouble with the Blue Hole Pool Company. They have my money, but I don't yet have a pool—nor does it look as if I will get one anytime soon. I have written several letters demanding either action or explanation, with no result.

My patience is beginning to wear thin. I'd appreciate any help or advice you could offer. Thank you.

Sincerely,

John Doe

Enclosures: Photocopied correspondence
Photocopied invoice

cc: Blue Hole Pool Co.

LEGAL HELP

Your complaint may reach the point where your only recourse is to begin legal proceedings. Again, you have several courses of action available. The first, and probably easiest, is to have your attorney or a legal aid service write a letter to the company or individual who is the source of your problem. This may be enough to stimulate action.

Another option is small claims court. If the amount in dispute is small (the amount varies from state to state), you may file suit in small claims court. Court fees are usually nominal, and in many cases your filing fees are refunded if you win the case. The decision of the judge is binding. The drawback to this procedure is the amount of time it takes. Nonetheless, you can get satisfaction if your facts are correct and you pursue your case intelligently.

Finally, if your problem seems resolvable by no other means, you may decide to have an attorney pursue the matter for you—even to the point of filing suit. That, however, is beyond the scope of this book. Complaints requiring the services of an attorney are usually large to begin with—larger than you would normally address in a complaint letter. Even for these large amounts, going to court is a lot of trouble—an experience most people would prefer to avoid if at all possible.

Present your case in a reasonable, well-written letter, and you'll probably never have to worry about that.

SUMMARY

The theory behind the third-party strategy is threefold: In the first place, the company or individual to whom you're complaining can see that you don't intend to give up until you are satisfied. Second, receiving letters and phone calls from various law enforcement agencies, consumer organizations, and media representatives may convince the offending party to give in before things get out of hand.

Third, in the words of Don Nagle, whom we met earlier in this chapter, the idea is to "wear the guy down." If everyone is writing to him and calling him, and he finds he is spending the whole day dealing with your complaint, he may decide it is time to cut his losses and give in to you.

The point is, third parties can be used to tremendous advantage. Because of that, it can be tempting to resort to them too quickly. We would caution you to use them wisely and cautiously. Do as much as you can on your own before you ask for outside assistance. Your call for help will be that much more credible.

Used wisely, third parties are your final and most effective asset.

A Final Word

By now it should be clear that getting a complaint taken care of is actually a fairly simple matter. We've shown you how to write an effective complaint letter, and where to direct it. We've demonstrated how to strengthen your tone if a second letter is necessary, and how to effectively use the "cc." Finally, we've shown you where to go for outside help if you need it.

Our tone throughout this book has been serious, because most complaints are serious. However, not every complaint involves large amounts of money or serious inconvenience. There are times when humor can be used to advantage. Here's our favorite example:

A few years ago David Cormier, a retired army colonel, found a piece of string baked into one of his favorite snacks. He sent the following letter off to the manufacturer, along with the faulty cracker:

Complaint Department
American Cracker Co.
Paramus, NJ 07652

Dear Sirs:

Stix with my sandwich,

Stix with my soup,

Stix for a snack are divine.

But if you will,

Dear Amcracko, please,

I'd prefer my Stix . . . without twine.

Respectfully yours,

David Cormier

Mr. Cormier received a response from the company a few days later. The letter apologized for the problem and then went on to thank the colonel for his delightful letter. It was being circulated throughout the company and everyone was enjoying his poem.

Weeks later a representative of the company called and asked if he could come by to meet Mr. Cormier in person. When the representative arrived, he brought not only a letter of appreciation, but also several cases of Stix and other crackers and cookies!

We can't guarantee this kind of response every time, but go ahead and use humor if it seems appropriate.

Whatever way you handle your complaint, we leave you with this advice: Don't settle for less than what you paid for, or what you expect. Stand up for your rights as a consumer! If enough of us do this, the quality of merchandise and service in this country can improve for everyone!

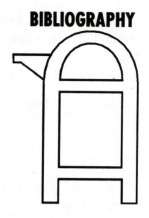

BIBLIOGRAPHY

BIBLIOGRAPHY
AND
RESOURCES

There's more to know about effective writing—of complaint letters or other correspondence—than can be included in one book. For more information, refer to this list of useful reference manuals and books on writing techniques.

Style Guides

The Chicago Manual of Style. 14th ed. Chicago: The University of Chicago Press, 1993.

Strunk, William, Jr., and E. B. White. *The Elements of Style.* 3d ed. New York: Macmillan, 1979.

Jordan, Lewis. *The New York Times Manual of Style and Usage.* New York: Times Books, 1976.

Bernstein, Theodore M. *The Careful Writer.* New York: Atheneum, 1985.

Follett, Wilson. *Modern American Usage.* New York: Hill and Wang, 1966.

Grammer References

Hairston, Maxine, and John J. Ruszkiewicz. *The Scott, Foresman Handbook for Writers.* Glenview, Illinois: Scott, Foresman and Company, 1988.

Hodges, John C., Winifred Bryan Horner, Suzanne Strobeck Webb, and Robert Keith Miller, *Harbrace College Handbook.* 12th ed. Fort Worth: Harcourt Brace College Publishers, 1994.

Ebbitt, Wilma R., and David R. Ebbitt, *Writer's Guide and Index to English.* 7th ed. Glenview, Illinois: Scott, Foresman and Company, 1972.

Sabin, William A. *The Gregg Reference Manual,* 6th ed. New York: Gregg Division/McGraw-Hill, 1985.

Warriner, John E., May Whitten, and Francis Griffith. *English Grammar and Composition.* New York: Harcourt Brace Jovanovich, 1977.

Writing References

Booher, Dianna. *Would You Put That In Writing?* New York: Facts On File, Inc., 1983.

DeVries, Mary A. *The New American Handbook Of Letter Writing.* New York: Signet Reference, 1988.

Elbow, Peter. *Writing With Power.* New York: Oxford University Press, 1981.

Fruehling, Rosemary T., and N. B. Oldham. *Write To The Point: Letters, Memos, and Reports That Get Results.* New York: McGraw-Hill, 1988.

Tietz, Robert, and Elaine Tietz. *Complete Book Of Effective Personal Letters.* New York: Prentice-Hall, 1984.

Westheimer, Patricia H. *The Perfect Memo.* Glenview, Illinois: Scott, Foresman and Company, 1988.

Westheimer, Patricia H. *Power Writing for Executive Women.* Glenview, Illinois Scott, Foresman and Company, 1989.

Westheimer, Patricia H., and Robert B. Nelson. *The Perfect Letter.* Glenview, Illinois: Scott, Foresman and Comapny, 1990.

Westheimer, Patricia H., and Jacqueline S. Senteney. *The Executive Style Book.* Glenview, Illinois: Scott, Foresman and Company, 1988.

Westheimer, Patricia H., and Julie Wheatcroft. *Grammar for Business.* Glenview, Illinois: Scott, Foresman and Company, 1990.

Williams, Joseph M. *Style: Ten Lessons in Clarity & Grace.* Glenview, Illinois: Scott, Foresman and Company, 1981.

APPENDIX

A

Sample Letters

COMPLAINT LETTER FORMAT AND RULES

Today's date, year

Your Name
Your Address
Your City, State, ZIP Code

Mr./Mrs.
Title
Company Name
Company Address
City, State, ZIP Code

Dear Mr./Ms.
    [State your loss or inconvenience as succinctly as possible. Avoid emotionalism and stick to the facts. State the action you expect. If you believe the company owes you a new product or free service, say so.]

    [Use a positive tone if possible. Angry, rude letters get negative, defensive reactions. Give a specific explanation of the problem. Use amounts, dates, model numbers, and any other pertinent information. Keep your letter to one page. Instead of summarizing other letters or phone calls, make copies and enclose them.]

    [Close in a friendly, positive manner. Assure the reader that you trust the individual and fully expect that person to help you. Follow up on the phone, but be sure and tell the reader when you intend to call.]

Sincerely,

Your Name (and signature above)

Enclosures (if included)

cc: (if copies mailed—state to whom)

LESS EFFECTIVE

Dear Mr. Smith:

Please find enclosed a copy of your invoice number 2283, as of 23 July 1993. Be advised that we will be unable to effect remuneration of this invoice pending your completion of the work delineated in our contractual agreement. In particular, installation of the workspace delimiters is critical if we are to operationalize our accounts/receivable department. Pending outcome of this contract and the work described therein, your continued association with this firm remains under advisement.

Sincerely,

Mr. Jones

MORE EFFECTIVE

Dear Mr. Smith:

Here's a copy of your invoice (#2283) dated July 23, 1993. I'm afraid we must withhold payment on this invoice until you complete the work listed in our contract. We would like you to install the room dividers immediately so that our accounting department can begin work.

If you do not complete this job soon, we may not call on you for our future needs.

Sincerely,

Mr. Jones

LESS EFFECTIVE

Dear Sirs:

Once again I tried flying your airline. Once again, Midcountry did not let me down. You lost my luggage, and you changed planes on me. My seat— assigned a month earlier—was eliminated, and I had to move from the business class to a center seat in the smoking section. I did have a choice, of course. I could have waited for the next flight and missed a business meeting. Missing that meeting would have cost my company about $3,000,000.00. Has anyone ever sued an airline company for money lost because of a missed meeting due to your lack of concern for your customers?

In our company we do excessive business travel, and the word is that Midcountry is not a company to be trusted. We avoid using Midcountry as much as possible. I think a reevaluation of your service and attention given to your customers is in order.

Sincerely,

Robert Helms
Vice President
Singelton Data Products

Dear Mr. Pender:

My last flight on your airline was unsatisfactory. You delivered me to my destination, but under conditions quite different from those specified in our contract (the ticket). Therefore, I would like you to refund at least half the purchase price of my ticket ($458.00).

This is what happened: First, after reserving and paying for a business-class ticket a month in advance, I found that you had changed planes, and my reserved seat no longer existed. I was shuffled to the smoking section in the back of the plane. I didn't have much choice. Had I waited for the next flight, I would have missed an important business meeting—at a potential loss to my company of $3,000,000.00.

Second, you lost my luggage—and this is not the first time that has happened. Frankly, I am becoming discouraged with the service you provide. Executives of my company travel extensively, and we have used Midcountry frequently in the past. However, unless your service improves, we will be forced to avoid your airline in the future.

For now, I look forward to an apology and a check for $229.00.

Sincerely,

Robert Helms
Vice President
Singelton Data Products

LESS EFFECTIVE

Dear Ms. Dewar:

On Monday, February 14, 1994 I purchased my new car from your dealership. At that time I agreed to purchase a car with a factory installed cassette deck. The car I took possession of (serial #1288634) did not have a cassette deck. Therefore, the dealership agreed to replace the stereo with a stereo/cassette deck. Please see the enclosed copy of the Equipment, Condition, and Warranty Release signed by Mr. Simpson and myself. At that time I was very pleased with both my purchase and the way I had been treated at your dealership.

Unfortunately, a number of things have happened since then that have altered this pleasure. I still enjoy my car and believe it is a fine product. This is my second car from your company. However, unless I obtain *both* a cassette deck and, more importantly, an explanation for the way I have been treated as a customer, I have no recourse but to have my car serviced at another dealership, to purchase any other cars from another dealership, to announce and publicize my acute displeasure with the way I have been treated by Dewar Motors, and to begin legal proceedings.

I have recorded the specific details of the problems I have encountered dealing with your employees, and have enclosed a copy of this record for your information. I also would like to point out that I received polite and courteous help from only the saleswoman, Ms. Robinson and from the service advisor Ms. Olsen. Unfortunately, it was apparent that neither of these people had the authority to make any final decisions. In contrast, the other people I dealt with, including Mr. Goodwin and Mr. Williams, whom I perceived had the authority to help me, were evasive and rude. Furthermore, in my last conversation with Mr. Williams on April 6, 1993, he was vindictive, vulgar and verbally abusive with me.

I hope that this conflict can be resolved as quickly as possible in a more productive and adult manner. I am awaiting your reply.

Sincerely,

Helen Moresby

MORE EFFECTIVE

Dear Ms. Dewar:

Until now, I have been happy with the service I have received from your dealership. I am no longer. I have waited nearly two months for a cassette deck to be installed, and I feel I have waited long enough. I'm asking you to see to it that the player is installed by Friday of next week. Further, I demand a written apology from your sales manager, Mr. Williams.

I purchased my Ford Taurus from your dealership on February 14 of this year, and I am quite pleased with it. I am also pleased with the courteous attention given me by Ms. Olsen and Ms. Robinson. However, I am very displeased with the treatment I've received from Mr. Goodwin and, in particular, Mr. Williams. He has consistently refused to give me the service I paid for. And the last time I spoke with him, Mr. Williams was vulgar and verbally abusive toward me.

Ms. Dewar, this is no way to treat a steady customer such as myself. In the past two months, I've endured numerous phone calls, several wasted trips to your dealership, and vindictive insults. I'm confident that, had you been aware of my situation earlier, none of this would have happened.

Now that you do know, I am certain that my cassette deck will be installed promptly and that my unpleasant experience with your employees will not be repeated.

I look forward to hearing from you by May 1.

Sincerely,

Ellen Moresby

LESS EFFECTIVE

Dear Mr. Hansen:

I ordered three Nelson E-2 focusing screens on April 24, 1993 and received them on May 10, 1993. When I opened the box of one of the focusing screens, I noticed the screen was not placed in the plastic container correctly. It was loosely held off to the right side of the container instead of sitting snugly in the bed made to hold it. Upon further inspection, I noticed the focusing screen was scratched on the bottom left. Therefore, I am returning the scratched focusing screen as I found it, and would like another undamaged E-2 focusing screen sent to replace it. The other two focusing screens were in perfect condition. Thank you.

I called to get return authorization this morning. Bob Kendall told me to send the focusing screen, along with a letter and a copy of the packing receipt (which I've enclosed), and he said the screen would be exchanged. Please send the new E-2 focusing screen as soon as possible. Thanks for your time.

Sincerely,

Nancy Powell

MORE EFFECTIVE

Dear Mr. Hansen:

Thank you for the prompt delivery of the three Nelson E-2 focusing screens I ordered on April 23, 1993. I received them on May 10, 1993.

Unfortunately, when I opened one of the boxes, I found that the focusing screen within had a large scratch on its bottom left corner. I am returning the damaged screen as I found it, and I would like another undamaged E-2 focusing screen sent in its place. The other two screens were in perfect condition.

I called to get return authorization this morning. Bob Kendall told me to return the damaged screen, along with a letter and a copy of the packing receipt, which I've enclosed. He said the screen would be exchanged and a new screen sent as soon as possible.

I appreciate this prompt and courteous service and look forward to doing more business with you.

Sincerely,

Nancy Powell

Dear General Manager:

I ordered a Nikkor AIS non-autofocus 28mm (2.8) lens, a lens case, and a 52mm L37C filter from your store on April 2, 1993. I have since received my Visa card statement, which shows that a transaction for $209.35 was made on April 12, 1993, for the above items ordered. So, you have my money. My question is this: Where is my photo equipment? It has been over 30 days since I ordered the stuff!

According to *Photography News,* "the advertiser (that's you) must ship the merchandise within 30 days after the receipt of a phone order (that's me). If an advertiser cannot ship the merchandise within the required delivery time, it must notify the customer (that's me again) by mail immediately of the revised shipping date. The reply card must give the customer the option of canceling the order or accepting the delay."

I know you guys in New York are very, very busy, but please give me just a little customer courtesy and let me know what's happening with my "merchandise" (and *please* don't tell me "the computers are down"). Thanks so very much for your precious time, and I look forward to hearing from you within 10 business days (otherwise, *Photography News will* just have to read this letter).

Sincerely,

Laura Gomez

MORE EFFECTIVE

Dear General Manager:

It is important that I know the status of several items I ordered from your store last month. It has been over 50 days since I placed the order, yet I have not received the merchandise, nor have I received a revised shipping date from you.

On April 2, 1993, I ordered a Nikkor AIS non-autofocus 28mm (2.8) lens, a lens case, and a 62mm L37C filter from your store. On April 17 I received a Visa card statement showing a transaction for $209.35, made on April 12, 1993 for the ordered items.

As I'm sure you're aware, the *Photography News* policy concerning mail order advertising states, in part, "...the advertiser must ship the merchandise within 30 days after the receipt of a phone or mail order. If an advertiser cannot ship the merchandise within the required delivery time, it must notify the customer by mail immediately of the revised shipping date and must include a self-addressed, postage-paid reply card. The reply card must give the customer the option of canceling the order or accepting the delay."

Please adhere to these guidelines. I have called twice for information, and your salespeople have rebuffed me each time. I will be traveling abroad next month, and it is critical that I know promptly the status of this equipment.

Thank you.

Sincerely,

Laura Gomez

Mr. Patterson:

We were guests in your hotel last week, and it was one of the worst experiences of our lives. I awoke in the middle of the night to the smell of smoke. When I opened our door and looked into the hallway, it was filled with smoke. I never heard any alarm! I woke my wife, and we made our way outside.

What kind of establishment are you running? Do you have no concern at all for your guests' lives? Why weren't the fire alarms working? We could have been killed, along with many other people. When we checked out, your clerk made no apology, nor would she have even mentioned the fire had we not brought it up. She seemed to think it was funny!

I think you are guilty of criminal neglect. We will never stay at your hotel again, and we will warn all of our friends. I am considering suing you and your company. As near as I can figure, you must be some kind of idiot, or else you don't care about the lives of your guests. If you did, you'd fix the fire alarms!

Disgusted,

John Forrester

MORE EFFECTIVE

Dear Mr. Patterson:

I am very upset about our experience as guests of your hotel on March 8, 1993. As a result, I believe you should refund our money for that night. A copy of your bill for $95 is enclosed.

On that night, my wife and I awoke to the smell of smoke. We made our way quickly through the smoke-filled hallway to the stairwell and finally outside. At no time did we hear an alarm. When we checked out the next morning, there was no apology for the inconvenience, not to mention the threat to our lives and health.

I'm sure you realize the potential for tragedy in a situation like that. I strongly recommend that you investigate the status of your fire and smoke alarms, and that you ensure they will work in any future incidents. In the meantime, I will expect my check for $95.

Sincerely,

John Forrester

LESS EFFECTIVE

Dear Ms. Kokes:

Because your delivery of premium and regular channels is far below normal and acceptable standards, I hope to petition the Federal Communications Commission to revoke your franchise for Ines County.

I have been paying dearly for a subscription service, and it is the generally accepted business practice of a subscription commodity not to charge for nondelivery.

Not one week has gone by without major service interruptions or nondelivery. Last evening we had the opportunity to view all of about four channels. I could do better with an antenna.

I'm paying more than $650 annually, and what I'm paying for is enhanced signal delivery and entertainment channels. I'm not receiving either consistently.

If service does not improve significantly, I will cancel my service. I shall also petition the FCC for a rebate on nondelivered subscription service. Every time I call your Bakersfield office, I'm told, "We have a problem in Valley Park, but we're working on it." It seems you've been working on it for about three years now.

Disappointedly,

Ron Miller

MORE EFFECTIVE

Dear Ms. Kokes:

I'm very unhappy with the service I have received from your company. I would like your personal guarantee that I will be receiving all of the fifteen channels I am paying for—and consistently—by June 12, 1993. If this is not possible, I wish to have my fees for January through May, 1993, a total of $285, refunded in full.

For the past three years I have paid for enhanced reception and entertainment channels, neither of which I have received consistently. Last night I was able to view only four channels. I'm certain I could do better with an antenna. Each time I call your office, I'm told, "There is a problem, but we're working on it."

That is not acceptable. Please let me know if you will be able to provide the service you promise. Otherwise, cancel my account and refund my money so that I may take my business elsewhere.

Thank you. I look forward to hearing from you by June 12.

Sincerely,

Ron Miller

APPENDIX

B

Third Party Agencies and Organizations

The information in Appendix B is published through the courtesy of the U.S. Office of Consumer Affairs in Washington D.C.

These are only a representative sample of pages from their publications. Additional information listing corporate consumer contacts, automobile manufacturers, federal agencies, state utility commissions, and state, county, and city government consumer protection offices is also available. We recommend you request a recent, comprehensive list from the Consumer Information Center in Pueblo, CO 81009.

Their phone number is 1-719-948-3334.

BETTER BUSINESS BUREAUS

National Headquarters

Council of Better Business Bureaus, Inc.
4200 Wilson Boulevard, Suite 800
Arlington, VA 22203
(703) 276-0100

Local Bureaus

Alabama
P.O. Box 55268
Birmingham, AL 35205
(205) 558-2222

P.O. Box 383
Huntsville, AL 35804
(205) 533-1640

707 Van Antwerp Building
Mobile, AL 36602
(205) 433-5494, 5495

Alaska
4011 Artic Boulevard
Anchorage, AK 99503
(907) 562-0704

Arizona
4428 North 12th Street
Phoenix, AZ 85014
(602) 264-1721

3620 N. 1st Street, Suite 118
Tuscon, AZ 85719
(602) 888-5353

Arkansas
1415 South University
Little Rock, AR 72204
(501) 664-7274

California
705 Eighteenth Street
Bakersfield, CA 93301
(805) 322-2074

290 North 10th Street, Suite 206
Colton, CA 92324
(714) 527-0608

6101 Ball Road, Suite 309
Cyprus, CA 92630
(714) 527-0680

1398 W. Indianapolis, Suite 102
Fresno, CA 93705
(209) 222-8111

3400 W. 6th Street
Los Angeles, CA 90020
(213) 251-9696

510 16th Street, Suite 550
Oakland, CA 94612
(510) 238-1000

400 South Street
Sacramento, CA 95814
(916) 443-6843

3111 Camino Del Rio, Suite 600
San Diego, CA 92108
(619) 521-5898

33 New Montgomery Tower, Suite 290
San Francisco, CA 94105
(415) 243-9999

1530 Meridian Avenue, #100
San Jose, CA 95125
(408) 445-3000

400 S. El Camino Royale
San Mateo, CA 94402
(415) 696-1240

P.O. Box 746
Santa Barbara, CA 93102
(805) 963-8657

1111 North Center Street
Stockton, CA 95202
(209) 948-8657

Colorado
3022 N. El Paso
Colorado Springs, CO 80907
(719) 636-1155

1780 South Bellaire, Suite 700
Denver, CO 80222
(303) 758-2100

1730 S. College Avenue, Suite 303
Fort Collins, CO 80524
(303) 484-1348

119 West 6th Street, Suite 203
Pueblo, CO 81003
(719) 542-6464

Connecticut
Fairfield Woods Plaza
2345 Black Rock Turnpike
Fairfield, CT 06430
(203) 374-6161

100 South Turnpike Road
Wallingford, CT 06492
(203) 269-2700

Delaware
2055 Limestone Road
P.O. Box 5361
Wilmington, DE 19808
(302) 996-9200

District of Columbia
1012 14th Street, N.W., 14th Floor
Washington, DC 20005
(202) 393-8000

Florida
5830 142nd Avenue, North #B
P.O. Box 7950
Clearwater, FL 34618
(813) 854-1154

2976 E. Cleveland Avenue
Fort Myers, FL 33901
(813) 334-7331

16291 North West 57th Avenue
Miami, FL 33014
1-900-225-2552 (average call $3.80)

400 Alcomiz Street
Pensacola, FL 32501
(904) 433-6111

2247 Palm Beach Lake Boulevard
West Palm Beach, FL 33409
(305) 686-2200

1011 Wymore Road, Suite 204
Winter Park, FL 32789
(407) 621-3300

Georgia
100 Edgewood Avenue, Suite 1012
Atlanta, GA 30303
(404) 688-4910

624 Ellis Street, Suite 106
Augusta, GA 30901
(706) 722-1574

8 13th Street
Columbus, GA 31901
(404) 324-0712

6606 Albercorn Street, Suite 108C
Savannah, GA 31416
(912) 354-7521

Hawaii
1600 Kapiolani Boulevard, Suite 714
Honolulu, HI 96813
(808) 942-2355

Idaho
1333 West Jefferson
Boise, ID 83702
(208) 342-4649

Illinois
211 West Wacker Drive
Chicago, IL 60606
(312) 444-1188

3024 W. Lake
Peoria, IL 61615
(309) 688-3741

Indiana
722 W. Bristol Street
Elkhart, IN 46514
(219) 262-8996

4004 Morgan Avenue, Suite 201
Evansville, IN 47715
(812) 473-0202

1203 Webster Street
Fort Wayne, IN 46802
(219) 423-4433

4231 Cleveland Street
Gary, IN 46408
(219) 980-1511

Victoria Centre
22 East Washington Street
Suite 200
Indianapolis, IN 46204
(317) 637-0197

Ball State University
BBB Whitinger Building, Room 150
Muncie, IN 47306
(317) 285-5669

52303 Emmons Road
Suite 9
South Bend, IN 46637
(219) 277-9121

Iowa
852 Middle Road
Bettendorf, IA 52722
(319) 355-6344

615 Insurance Exchange Building
Des Moines, IA 50309
(515) 243-8137

318 Badgerow Building
Sioux City, IA 51101
(712) 252-4501

Kansas
501 Jefferson
Suite 24
Topeka, KS 66607
(913) 232-0454

300 Kaufman Building
Wichita, KS 67202
(316) 263-3146

Kentucky
311 W. Short Street
Lexington, KY 40203
(606) 259-1008

844 South Fourth Street
Louisville, KY 40203
(502) 583-6546

Louisiana

1605 Murray Street
Suite 117
Alexandria, LA 71301
(318) 473-4494

2055 Wooddale Boulevard
Baton Rouge, LA 70806
(504) 926-3010

501 E. Main Street
Houma, LA 70360
(504) 868-3456

100 Huggins Road
P.O. Box 30297
Lafayette, LA 70593
(318) 981-3497

3941 Ryan Street
P.O. Box 7314
Lake Charles, LA 70605
(318) 478-6253

141 De Siard Street
Suite 300
Monroe, LA 71201
(318) 387-4600

1539 Jackson Avenue
New Orleans, LA 70130
(504) 581-6222

3612 Youree Drive
Shreveport, LA 71105
(318) 861-6417

Maine

812 Stevens Avenue
Portland, ME 04103
(207) 878-2715

Maryland

2100 Huntingdon Avenue
Baltimore, MD 21211
(301) 347-3990

Massachusetts

20 Park Plaza
Suite 820
Boston, MA 02108
(617) 426-9000

293 Bridge Street
Suite 320
Springfield, MA 01103
(413) 734-3114

32 Franklin Street
Worcester, MA 01608
(508) 755-2548

Michigan

620 Trust Building
Grand Rapids, MI 49503
(616) 774-8236

30555 S. Field Road
Southfield, MI 48076
(810) 644-9100

Minnesota

2706 Gannon Road
St. Paul, MN 55116
(612) 699-1111

Mississippi
460 Briarwood Drive
Suite 340
Jackson, MS 39206
(601) 956-8282

Missouri
306 East 12th Street
Suite 1024
Kansas City, MO 64106
(816) 421-7800

5100 Oakland, Suite 200
St. Louis, MO 63110
(314) 531-3300

205 Park Central East
Suite 509
Springfield, MO 65806
(417) 862-4222

Nebraska
719 North 48th Street
Lincoln, NE 68504
(402) 467-5261

2210 N. 91st Plaza
Omaha, NE 68134
(402) 391-7612

Nevada
1022 E. Sierra Avenue
Las Vegas, NV 89104
(702) 735-6900

991 Bible Way
Reno, NV 89515
(702) 322-0657

New Hampshire
410 S. Main Street
Concord, NH 03301
(603) 224-1991

New Jersey
494 Broadway Street
Newark, NJ 07102
(201) 642-4636

2 Forest Avenue
Paramus, NJ 07652
(201) 845-4044

1721 Route 37 East
Toms River, NJ 08753
(201) 270-5577

1700 Whitehorse Hamilton Square
Suite D-5
Trenton, NJ 08690
(609) 588-0808

16 Maple Avenue
Box 303
Westmont, NJ 08108
(609) 854-8467

New Mexico
2625 Pennsylvania NE
Suite 2050
Albuquerque, NM 87109
(505) 884-0500

308 North Locke
Farmington, NM 87110
(505) 326-6501

New York

346 Delaware Avenue
Buffalo, NY 14202
(716) 856-7180

257 Park Avenue, South
New York, NY 10010
1-900-463-6222
(.95 charge per minute)

847 James Street
Suite 200
Syracuse, NY 13202
(315) 479-6635

30 Glenn Street
White Plains, NY 10603
(914) 428-1230

North Carolina

801 BB&T Building
Ashville, NC 28801
(704) 253-2392

5200 Park Road
Suite 202
Charlotte, NC 28209
(704) 527-0012

3608 West Friendly Avenue
Greensboro, NC 27410
(919) 852-4240

3120 Poplarwood Court
Suite 101
Raleigh, NC 27604
(919) 872-9240

500 West 5th Street, Suite 202
Winston-Salem, NC 27101
(919) 725-8348

Ohio
222 W. Market Street
Akron, OH 44303
(216) 253-4590

898 Walnut Street
Cincinnati, OH 45202
(513) 421-3015

1335 Dublin Road
Suite 30-A
Columbus, OH 43215
(614) 486-6336

40 West Fourth Street
Suite 1250
Dayton, OH 45402
(513) 222-5825

130 W. 2nd Street
Mansfield, OH 44902
(419) 522-1700

425 Jefferson Avenue, Suite 909
Toledo, OH 43604
(419) 241-6276

311 Mahoning Bank Building
Youngstown, OH 44501
(216) 744-3111

Oklahoma
17 South Dewey
Oklahoma City, OK 73102
(405) 239-6081

6711 S. Yale, Suite 230
Tulsa, OK 74136
(918) 492-1266

Oregon
520 S.W. Alder Street
Suite 615
Portland, OR 97205
(503) 226-3981

Pennsylvania
528 North New Street
Bethlehem, PA 18018
(215) 866-8780

6 Marion Court
Lancaster, PA 17602
1-800-220-8032

1930 Chestnut Street
P.O. Box 2297
Philadelphia, PA 19103
(215) 496-1000

610 Smithfield Street
Pittsburgh, PA 15222
(412) 456-2700

P.O. Box 993
Scranton, PA 18501
(717) 342-9129

Puerto Rico
GPO Box 70212
San Juan, PR 00936
(809) 756-5402

Rhode Island
Bureau Park, Box 1300
Warrick, RI 02887
(401) 785-1212

South Carolina
1830 Bull Street
Columbia, SC 29201
(803) 254-2525

113 Mills Avenue
Greenville, SC 29605
(803) 242-5052

Tennessee
1010 Market Street
Suite 200
Chattanooga, TN 37402
(615) 266-6144

2633 Kingston Pike #2
P. O. 1327
Knoxville, TN 37939
(615) 522-2552

3792 S. Mendenhall
Memphis, TN 38115
(901) 795-8771

1 Commerce Place
Suite 1830
Nashville, TN 37239
(615) 254-5872

Texas
3300 S. 14th Street
Suite 307
Abilene, TX 79605
(915) 691-1533

P.O. Box 1905
Amarillo, TX 79105
(806) 379-6222

2101 S. I-H 35, Suite 302
Austin, IX 78741
(512) 445-2911

476 Oakland Avenue
Beaumont, TX 77704
(409) 835-5348

202 Varisco Building
Bryan, TX 77803
(409) 823-8148

2001 Bryan Street, Suite 850
Dallas, TX 75201
(214) 220-2000

1612 Summit Avenue #1260
Fort Worth, TX 76102
(817) 332-7585

2707 North Loop West
Houston, TX 77008
(713) 868-9500

1206 14th Street #901
Lubbock, TX 97401
(806) 763-0459

P.O. Box 60206
Midland, TX 79711
(915) 563-1880

3121 Executive Drive
San Angelo, TX 76904
(915) 949-2989

1800 Northeast Loop 410
Suite 400
San Antonio, TX 78217
(512) 828-9441

6801 Sanger
Suite 125
Waco, TX 76710
(817) 772-7530

P.O. Box 69
Weslaco, TX 78596
(512) 968-3678

1106 Brook Avenue
Wichita Falls, TX 76301
(817) 723-5526

Utah
1588 South Main Street
Salt Lake City, UT 84115
(801) 487-4656

Virginia
3608 Tidewater Drive
Norfolk, VA 23509
(804) 627-5651

701 East Franklin Street
Suite 712
Richmond, VA 23219
(804) 648-0016

31 W. Campbell Avenue
Roanoke, VA 24011
(703) 342-3455

Washington

101 N. Union #105
Kennewick, WA 99336
(509) 783-0892

4800 S. 1885th Street #222
Seattle, WA 98188
(206) 431-2222

South 176 Stevens
Spokane, WA 99204
(509) 747-1155

1101 Fawcett Avenue, #222
Tacoma, WA 98402
(206) 383-5561

P. O. Box 1584
Yakima, WA 98907
(509) 248-1326

Wisconsin

740 North Plankinton Avenue
Milwaukee, Wl 53203
(414) 273-1600

TRADE ASSOCIATIONS AND THIRD-PARTY DISPUTE RESOLUTION PROGRAMS

Public Relations
American Ambulance Association
1301 Connecticul Ave. N.W.
Washington, DC 20036
(202) 887-5144

Membership: Private providers of pre-hospital medical care and medical transportation.

Director, Education and Conventions
American Apparel Manufacturers Association
2500 Wilson Boulevard, Suite 301
Arlington, VA 22201
(703) 524-1864

Membership: Manufacturers of wearing apparel.

Public Relations Director
American Arbitration Association
140 West 51st Street
New York, NY 10020
(212) 484-4006

Membership: Arbitrators

Member Relations
American Automobile Association
12600 Fairlake Circle
Fairfax, VA 22033
(703) 222-4200

Membership: Federation of automobile clubs.

Director of Public Relations
American Collectors Association
4040 West 70th Street,
P. O. Box 39106
Minneapolis, MN 55435
(612) 926-6547

Membership: Collection services handling overdue accounts
for retail, professional, and commercial credit grantors.

Information Department
**American Council of Life Insurance/Health
Insurance Association of America**
1001 Pennsylvania Avenue, N.W.
Washington, DC, 20004
(written inquiries only)

Membership: Life, accident, and health insurance companies
uthorized to do business in the United States.

Director, Consumer Affairs
Director, Community Affairs
American Gas Association
1515 Wilson Boulevard
Arlington, VA 22209
(703) 841-8583

Membership: Distributors and transporters of natural,
manufactured, and liquefied gas.

American Health Care Association
1201 L Street N.W.
Washington, D.C. 20005
(202) 842-4444

Membership: Federation of state associations of long-term health care facilities.

Director, Professional Ethics
American Institute of Certified Public Accountants
1211 Avenue of the Americas
New York, NY 10036
(212) 596-6200

Membership: Professional society of accountants certified by the states and territories.

Director, Consumer Affairs
American Society of Travel Agents, Inc.
1101 King Street
Alexandria, VA 22314
(703) 739-2782

Membership: Travel agents.

Director, Communications Division
American Textile Manufacturers Institute
1801 K Street N.W. #900
Washington, DC 20006
(202) 862-0552

Membership: textile mills operating machinery for the manufacturing and processing of cotton, man-made, wool, and silk textile products.

BBB AUTO LINE
Council of Better Business Bureaus
4200 Wilson Boulevard #800
Arlington, VA 22203
(703) 276-0100

Third-party dispute resolution program for AMC, Audi, General Motors and its divisions, Honda, Jeep, Nissan, Peugeot, Porsche, Renault, SAAB, and Volkswagen.

BBB National Consumer Arbitration Program
Council of Better Business Bureaus
4200 Wilson Boulevard #800
Arlington VA 22203
(703) 276-0100

Third-party dispute resolution.

Better Hearing Institute
P. O. Box 1840
Washington, DC 20013
(703) 642-0580
1 (800) EAR-WELL (toll free)

Membership: Professionals and others dedicated to helping persons with impaired hearing.

Consumer Affairs
Blue Cross and Blue Shield Association
1310 G Street N.W.
Washington, DC 20005
(202) 626-4780

Membership: Local Blue Cross and Blue Shield plans in the United States, Canada, and Jamaica.

Director of Governmental Affairs
Carpet and Rug Institute
1155 Connecticut Avenue N.W., #500
Washington, DC 20036
(written inquiries only)

Membership: Manufacturers of carpets, rugs, bath mats, and bedspreads; suppliers of raw materials and services to the industry.

Assistant Secretary
Cemetery Consumer Service Council
P. O. Box 3574
Washington, DC 20007
(703) 379-6426

Council members: The American Cemetery Association, Cremation Association of North America, and the Pre-Arrangement of Interment Association of America.

Chrysler Customer Arbitration Board
1200 Chrysler Dr.
Highland Park, WI 48288
1-800-992-1997

Director, Ethics and Consumer Affairs
Direct Marketing Association
6 East 43rd Street
New York, NY 10017
(written complaints only)

Membership: Members who market goods and services directly to consumers using direct mail, catalogs, telemarketing, magazine and newspaper ads, and broadcast advertising.

Code Administrator
Direct Selling Association
1666 K Street, N.W., #1010
Washington, DC 20006
(202) 293-5760

Membership: Manufacturers and distributors selling consumer products door-to-door and through home-party plans.

Manager, Consumer Affairs
Edison Electric Institute
701 Pennsylvania Avenue, N.W.
Washington, DC 20004
(202) 508-5000

Membership: Investor-owned electric utility companies
operating in the United States.

Executive Director, Consumer Affairs
Electronic Industries Association
Consumer Electronics Group
2001 Pennsylvania Avenue, N.W.
Washington, DC 20006
(202) 457-4977

Membership: Manufacturers of electronic parts, tubes, and
solid state components; radio, television and video systems;
audio equipment; and communications electronic products.

Ford Consumer Appeals Board
P.O. Box 51201
Southfield, MI 48086
1-800-392-3673 (toll free outside Michigan)

**Funeral Service Consumer Action Program
(ThanaCAP)**
11121 West Oklahoma Avenue
Milwaukee, WI 53227
(414) 541-2500

Third-party dispute resolution program sponsored by the
National Funeral Directors Association.

Director, Market Development
Hearing Industries Association
515 King Street #320
Alexandria, VA 22314
(703) 684-5744

Membership: Companies engaged in the manufacture and or sale of electronic hearing aids, their components, parts, and related products and services on a national basis.

Director, Consumer Affairs
Insurance Information Institute
110 William Street
New York, NY 10038
(212) 669-9200 (call collect in New York)
1-800-942-4242 (toll free outside New York)

Membership: Property and liability insurance companies.

National Headquarters
International Association for Financial Planning
2 Concourse Parkway
Suite 800
Atlanta, GA 30328
(404) 395-1605

Membership: Individuals involved in financial planning.

Director, Subscription Inquiry Service
Magazine Publishers Association
919 3rd Avenue
New York, NY 10022
(212) 752-0055
(written complaints only)

Membership: Publishers of 1,000 consumer and other magazines issued not less than three times a year.

Major Appliance Consumer Action Panel (MACAP)
20 North Wacker Drive
Chicago, IL 60606
(312) 984-5858
1 (800) 621-0477 (toll free outside Illinois)

Third-party dispute resolution program for the major appliance industry.

Executive Vice President
Monument Builders of North America
1740 Ridge Avenue
Evanston, IL 60201
(708) 869-2031

Membership: Monument retailers, manufacturers, and wholesalers; bronze manufacturers and suppliers.

Consumer Affairs Coordinator
Mortgage Bankers Association of America
1125 15th Street, N.W. 7th Floor
Washington, DC 20005
(202) 861-6583

Membership: Principal lending and investment interests in the mortgage finance field, including mortgage banking firms, commercial banks, life insurance companies, title companies, and savings and loan associations.

Multi-Door Dispute Resolution Program
500 Indiana Avenue, N.W. #1235
Washington, DC 20001
(202) 879-1549

(DC residents only)

National Advertising Division (NAD)
Council of Better Business Bureaus
845 Third Avenue
New York, NY 10022
(212) 754-1320

Program: Handles complaints about fraudulent and deceptive advertising.

Director, Consumer Affairs/Public Liaison
National Association of Home Builders
1201 15th Street, N.W.
Washington, DC 20005
(202) 822-0409

1 (800) 368-5242 (toll free outside District of Columbia)
Membership: Single and multi-family home builders,
commercial builders, and others associated with the building
industry.

National Association of Personnel Consultants
3133 Mt. Vernon Avenue
Alexandria, VA 22305
(703) 684-0180

Membership: Private employment agencies.

Consumer Arbitration Center
National Association of Securities Dealers, Inc.
33 Whitehall Street
New York City, NY 10004
(212) 858-4000

Third-party dispute resolution for complaints about over-the-
counter stocks and corporate bonds.

National Administrator
National Automotive Dealers Association
8400 Westpark Drive
McLean, VA 22101
(703) 821-7000

Third-party dispute resolution program administered through
the National Automotive Dealers Association.

Consumer Affairs
National Food Processors Association
1401 New York Avenue, N .W.
Washington, DC 20005
(202) 639-5939

Membership: Commercial packers of food products, such as
fruit, vegetables, meats, seafood, and canned, frozen,
dehydrated, pickled, and other preserved food items.

Manager, Compliance
National Futures Association
200 West Madison Street
Chicago, IL 60606
(312) 781-1410
1 (800) 621-3570 (toll free outside Illinois)

Membership: Futures commission merchants; commodity trading advisors; commodity pool operators; brokers and associated individuals.

Assistant to Executive Director
National Home Study Council
1601 18th Street, N.W.
Washington, DC 20009
(202) 234-5100
(written inquiries only)

Membership: Home study (correspondence) schools.

National Tire Dealers and Retreaders Association
1250 Eye Street, N.W. Suite 400
Washington, DC 20005
(202) 789-2300

Membership: Independent tire dealers and retreaders.

Department of Consumer Affairs
National Turkey Federation
11319 Sunset Hills Road
Reston, VA 22090
(written inquiries only)

Membership: Turkey growers, turkey hatcheries, turkey breeders, processors, marketers, and allied industry firms and poultry distributors.

Assistant Executive Director of Industry
Services and Communications
Photo Marketing Association
3000 Picture Place
Jackson, Ml 49201
(written complaints only)

Membership: Retailers of photo equipment, film, and supplies; firms developing and printing film.

Director of Consumer Affairs
The Soap and Detergent Association
475 Park Avenue South
New York, NY 10016
(212) 725-1262

Membership: Manufacturers of soap, detergents, fatty acids, and glycerine; raw materials suppliers.

Assistant Communications Director
Toy Manufacturers of America
200 Fifth Avenue
Room 740
New York, NY 10010
(212) 675-1141

Membership: American toy manufacturers.

President
U.S. Tour Operators Association (USTOA)
211 East 51st Street Suite 12-B
New York, NY 10022
(212) 750-7371

Membership: Wholesale tour operators, common carriers, suppliers, and purveyors of travel services.

STATE BANKING AUTHORITIES

Alabama
Superintendent of Banks
101S. Union
Montgomery, AL 36130
(205) 242-3452

Alaska
Director of Banking and Securities,
Pouch D
P.O. Box 110807
Juneau, AK 99811-0807
(907) 465-2521

Arizona
Superintendent of Banks
2910 N. 44th Street #310
Phoenix, AZ 85018
(602) 255-4421

Arkansas
Bank Commissioner
Tower Building
323 Center Street, Suite 500
Little Rock, AR 72201
(501) 324-9019

California
Superintendent of Banks
111 Pine Street #1100
San Francisco, CA 94111
(415) 557-3535

Colorado
State Bank Commissioner
Colorado Division of Banking
1560 Broadway #1175
Denver, CO 80202
(303) 894-7575

Connecticut
Banking Commissioner
44 Capitol Avenue
Hartford, CT 06106
(203) 566-4560

Delaware
State Bank Commissioner
555 E. Lookerman Street #210
Dover, DE 19901
(302) 739-4235

District of Columbia
Superintendent of Banking and Financial Institutions
441 4th Street, N.W., #1140 North
Washington, D.C. 20001
(202) 727-6365

Florida
State Comptroller
LL22
State Capitol Building
Tallahassee, FL 32399
(904) 488-0370

Georgia
Commissioner of Banking and Finance
2990 Brandywine Road, Suite 200
Atlanta, GA 30341
(404) 986-1633

Guam
Banking Commissioner
P.O. Box 2796
Agana, GU 96910
(written inquiries only)

Hawaii
Bank Examiner
P.O. Box 2045
Honolulu, HI 96805
(808) 586-2820

Idaho
Director, Dept. of Finance
700 West State Street, 2nd Floor
Boise, ID 83720
(208) 334-3319

Illinois
Commissioner of Banks and Trust Companies
500 E. Monroe, Room 400
Springfield, IL 62701
(217) 785-2837

Indiana
Director, Dept. of Financial Institutions
Indiana State Office Building
402 W. Washington Street
 Room 10066
Indianapolis, In 46204
(317) 232-3955

Iowa
Superintendent of Banking
200 East Grand
Suite 300
Des Moines, IA 50309
(515) 281-4014

Kansas
State Bank Commissioner
700 Jackson Street
Suite 300
Topeka, KS 66603
(913) 296-2266

Kentucky
Commissioner of Banking and Securities
477 Versailles Road
Frankfort, KY 40601
(502) 573-3390

Louisiana
Commissioner of Financial Institutions
P. O. Box 94095
Baton Rouge, LA 70804
(504) 925-4660

Maine
Superintendent of Banking
State House Station #36
Augusta, ME 04333
(207) 582-8713

Maryland
Bank Commissioner
501 St. Paul Place
Baltimore, MD 21202
(410) 333-6330

Massachusetts
Commissioner of Banks
100 Cambridge Street
Boston, MA 02202
(617) 727-3120

Michigan

Commissioner
Financial Institutions Bureau
P.O. Box 30224
Lansing, Ml 48909
(517) 373-3460

Minnesota

Deputy Commissioner of Commerce
133 E. 7th Street
St. Paul, MN 55101
(612) 296-2135

Mississippi

Commissioner
Dept. of Banking and Consumer Affairs
P.O. Box 23729
Jackson, MS 39225
(601) 359-1031

Missouri

Commissioner of Finance
P.O. Box 716
Jefferson City, MO 65102
(314) 751-3397

Montana

Commissioner of Financial Institutions
P.O. Box 200512
Helena, MT 59620
(406) 444-2091

Nebraska

Director of Banking and Finance
1200 N Street Atrium #311
Lincoln, NE 68508
(402) 471-2171

Nevada
Commissioner of Financial Institutions
406 East Second Street
Carson City, NV 89710
(702) 687-4259

New Hampshire
Bank Commissioner
169 Marchester Street
Concord, NH 03301
(603) 271-3561

New Jersey
Commissioner of Banking
20 West State Street
Trenton, NJ 08625
(609) 292-3420

New Mexico
Director, Financial Institutions Division
P.O. Box 25101
Santa Fe, NM 87504
(505) 827-7100

New York
Superintendent of Banks
Two Rector Street
New York, NY 10006
(212) 618-6642

North Carolina
Commissioner of Banks
P.O. Box 29512
Raleigh, NC 27626
(919) 733-3016

North Dakota
Commissioner of Banking and Financial Institutions
600 E. Boulevard Avenue
State Capitol, 13th Floor
Bismarck, ND 58505
(701) 224-2256

Ohio
Superintendent of Banks
77 S. High Street, 21st Floor
Columbus, OH 43266
(614) 466-2932

Oklahoma
Bank Commissioner
Malco Building
4100 North Lincoln Boulevard
Oklahoma City, OK 73105
(405) 521-2783

Oregon
Deputy Administrator
Financial Institutions Division
21 L & I Building
Salem, OR 97310
(503) 378-4140

Pennsylvania
Secretary of Banking
333 Market Street, 16th Floor
Harrisburg, PA 17101
(717) 787-6991

Puerto Rico
Commissioner of Banking
P. O. Box S4515
San Juan, PR 00905
(809) 721-5242

Rhode Island
Assistant Director
Banking and Securities
233 Richmond Street
Suite 231
Providence, RI 02903
(401) 277-2405

South Carolina
Commissioner of Banking
1015 Sumter Street
Room 309
Columbia, SC 29201
(803) 734-2001

South Dakota
Director of Banking and Finance
State Capital Building
550 E. Capital
Pierre, SD 57501
(605) 773-3421

Tennessee
Commissioner of Financial Institutions
John Sevier Building, 4th Floor
Nashville, TN 37243
(615) 741-2236

Texas
Banking Commissioner
2601 North Lamar
Austin, TX 78705
(512) 479-1200

Utah
Commissioner of Financial Institutions
P.O. Box 89
Salt Lake City, UT 84110
(801) 538-8830

Vermont
Commissioner of Banking and Insurance
89 Main Street, Drawer 20
Montpelier, VT 05620
(802) 828-3301

Virgin Islands
Lieutenant Governor
Chairman of the Banking Board
18 Kongens Gardens
P. O. Box 450
St. Thomas, VI 00802
(809) 774-2991

Virginia
Commissioner of Financial Institutions
P.O. Box 640
Richmond, VA 23205
(804) 371-9657

Washington
Supervisor of Banking
1400 Southeast Evergreen Park Dr. #120
Olympia, WA 98504
(206) 753-6520

West Virginia
Deputy Commissioner of Banking
State Office Building 3
Suite 311
Charleston, WV 25305
(304) 558-2294

Wisconsin
Commissioner of Banking
P. O. Box 7876
Madison, Wl 53707
(608) 266-1621

Wyoming
State Examiner
Herschler Building, 3rd Floor East
Cheyenne, WY 82002
(307) 777-6600

FEDERAL INFORMATION CENTERS

Alabama
Birmingham 1-800-366-2998
Mobile 1-800-366-2998

Alaska
Anchorage 1-800-729-8003

Arizona
Phoenix 1-800-359-3997

Arkansas
Little Rock 1-800-366-2998

California
Los Angeles 1-800-726-4995
Sacramento 1-800-726-4995
San Diego 1-800-726-4995
San Francisco 1-800-726-4995
Santa Ana 1-800-726-4995

Colorado
Colorado Springs 1-800-359-3997
Denver 1-800-359-3997
Pueblo 1-800-359-3997

Connecticut
Hartford 1-800-347-1997
New Haven 1-800-347-1997

Florida
Ft. Lauderdale 1-800-347-1997
Jacksonville 1-800-347-1997
Miami 1-800-347-1997
Orlando 1-800-347-1997
St. Petersburg 1-800-347-1997
Tampa 1-800-347-1997
West Palm Beach 1-800-347-1997

Georgia
Atlanta 1-800-347-1997

Hawaii
Honolulu 1-800-733-5996

Illinois
Chicago 1-800-366-2998

Indiana
Gary 1-800-366-2998
Indianapolis 1-800-347-1997

Iowa
From all points in Iowa
1-800-753-8004

Kansas
From all points in Kansas
1-800-735-8004

Kentucky
Louisville 1-800-347-1997

Louisiana
New Orleans 1-800-366-2998

Maryland
Baltimore 1-800-347-1997

Massachusetts
Boston 1-800-347-1997

Michigan
Detroit 1-800-347-1997
Grand Rapids 1-800-347-1997

Minnesota
Minneapolis 1-800-366-2998

Missouri
St. Louis 1-800-366-2998
From elsewhere in Missouri
1-800-735-8004

Nebraska
Omaha 1-800-366-2998
From elsewhere in Nebraska
1-800-735-8004

New Jersey
Newark 1-800-347-1997
Trenton 1-800-347-1997

New Mexico
Albuquerque 1-800-359-3997

New York
Albany 1-800-347-1997
Buffalo 1-800-347-1997
Rochester 1-800-347-1997
Syracuse 1-800-347-1997

North Carolina
Charlotte 1-800-347-1997

Ohio
Akron 1-800-347-1997
Cincinnati 1-800-347-1997
Cleveland 1-800-347-1997
Columbus 1-800-347-1997
Dayton 1-800-347-1997
Toledo 1-800-347-1997

Oklahoma
Oklahoma City 1-800-366-2998
Tulsa 1-800-366-2998

Oregon
Portland 1-800-726-4995

Pennsylvania
Philadelphia 1-800-347-1997
Pittsburgh 1-800-347-1997

Rhode Island
Providence 1-800-347-1997

Tennessee
Chattanooga 1-800-347-1997
Memphis 1-800-366-2998
Nashville 1-800-366-2998

Texas
Austin 1-800-366-2998
Dallas 1-800-366-2998
Fort Worth 1-800-366-2998
Houston 1-800-366-2998
San Antonio 1-800-366-2998

Utah
Salt Lake City 1-800-359-3997

Virginia
Norfolk 1-800-347-1997
Richmond 1-800-347-1997
Roanoke 1-800-347-1997

Washington
Seattle 1-800-726-4995
Tacoma 1-800-726-4995

Wisconsin
Milwaukee 1-800-366-2998

INDEX

-W-

More Good Books by JIST Works, Inc.

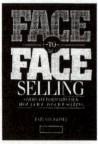

Face-To-Face Selling

By Bart Breightner

The author, founder and president of a successful art sales company, shares his unique sales success formula and talks straight about face-to-face selling. Entry-level salespeople will learn:

6 x 9, Paper, 223 pp.
ISBN 1-57112-065-3
$9.95 — Order Code FFS

- The art of convincing
- How to show a prospect the value of the product
- How to close the sale

Other Information:
- Tips on selling one-on-one and to groups
- Real-life examples of successful techniques
- Includes sound principles for effective phone work and a sample presentation

---

The Perfect Memo!

A Guide to Writing Memos with Confidence!
By Patricia H. Westheimer

This tutorial teaches readers how to organize their ideas and write clear memos. Introduces SPEAKWRITE™, a five-step approach to writing developed by the author during her more than 20 years as a business writing consultant.

6 x 9, Paper, 193 pp.
ISBN 1-57112-064-5
$12.95 — Order Code PM

Other Information:
- Highlights written communication skills that get results
- Transforms pompous writing into powerful prose
- Improves and refines business writing skills

Look for these and other fine books from **JIST Works, Inc.** at your full service bookstore, or call us for additional information at **800-648-5478**.

508454